Scott Rice is a profe~~~~~~~sh at San Jose State University and the cre~~~~~ the Bulwer-Lytton Contest. Born in Lewiston, Idaho, and raised in Spokane, Washington, he received his B.A. from Gonzaga University and his M.A. and Ph.D. from the University of Arizona. Scott Rice is married and the father of three children: Jeremy, Matthew, and Elizabeth. He is also the compiler of *It Was a Dark and Stormy Night* (available from Penguin).

Summer, 1986

*To Steve
on the occasion
of beginning his
first book: how
not to start.*

Judy

EDWARD BULWER-LYTTON

SON OF "IT WAS A DARK AND STORMY NIGHT"

More of the Best (?) from the Bulwer-Lytton Contest

Compiled by
SCOTT RICE

Penguin Books

PENGUIN BOOKS
Viking Penguin Inc., 40 West 23rd Street,
New York, New York 10010, U.S.A.
Penguin Books Ltd, Harmondsworth,
Middlesex, England
Penguin Books Australia Ltd, Ringwood,
Victoria, Australia
Penguin Books Canada Limited, 2801 John Street,
Markham, Ontario, Canada L3R 1B4
Penguin Books (N.Z.) Ltd, 182–190 Wairau Road,
Auckland 10, New Zealand

First published in Penguin Books 1986
Published simultaneously in Canada

The Apple logo used with the permission of Apple Computer, Inc.

CIP data available

Printed in the United States of America by
R. R. Donnelley & Sons, Harrisonburg, Virginia
Set in Caslon
Design by Beth Tondreau

CONTENTS

INTRODUCTION

The Bulwer-Lytton Fiction Contest is an annual competition sponsored by San Jose State University. It challenges entrants to compose the worst possible opening sentence to a hypothetical novel. The contest "honors" Edward George Bulwer-Lytton, a prolific Victorian novelist who opened his *Paul Clifford* (1830) with a sentence that has become the standard for potboilers: "It was a dark and stormy night . . ." Since the Bulwer-Lytton Fiction Contest became public in 1983, tens of thousands of irreverent scribblers have submitted sentences. A first collection of these appeared under the title *It Was a Dark and Stormy Night.* (Penguin Books. Available at your local book store. If it is not in stock, ask them to order you several copies.) Not content to leave well enough alone, we have decided to press our luck and publish *Son of "It Was a Dark and Stormy Night."* (Did you buy the last copy? If so, request your bookstore to reorder immediately.)

The first collection answered some of the standard questions raised by the contest. Since then, others have bobbed to the surface like . . . (fill in your own simile).

Q. Why do you persist in holding the Bulwer-Lytton Fiction Contest?

A. Because we believe that nothing is so powerful as a bad idea whose moment has come.

Q. Why would a university and an English department wish to associate themselves with a bad-writing contest?

A. That is a good question and we wish we had a good answer. As everyone knows, it is the proper business of universities to stage athletic contests and provide tailgate parties for alumni. Literary contests—of any kind—usually fall outside their sphere of interest, or at least their sphere of enthusiasm. In all fairness, though, you have to admit they have some cause. Can you imagine cluttering up a good fund-raising event with a bunch of impecunious literary types?

Q. Why would anyone want to enter a bad-writing contest?

A. Although the grand prize winners have received things such as word processors and have become virtual household names, people generally enter from a disinterested dedication to literacy. They expect nothing for themselves other than the satisfaction of knowing that they have done something to promote the cause of universal literacy and good taste.

Q. But don't you think that at least two or three might have entered out of some motive of personal gain?

A. Absolutely not. Literary people, professional and amateur, are animated only by the love of art and the prospect of bringing joy and optimism to others.

Q. Joy and optimism—even Samuel Beckett and Tennessee Williams?

A. Yes, especially them. Don't we all chuckle when we recall that hilarious moment at the end of *A Streetcar Named Desire* when they lead Blanche off to the asylum? And that merry funster Beckett—"Godot for it!"

Q. But what about Samuel Johnson? Didn't he say that no one but a blockhead ever wrote except for money?

A. Yes, and we have to respect that. After all, Johnson also said that a person who is tired of San Jose is tired of life. Still, a man of his kidney would hardly be able to foresee the apple-cheeked idealism that is rampant in the America of the '80s.

Q. Then the entrants are all literary idealists?

A. Yes. You have to understand that book people are a breed apart. They are untouched by the normal acquisitiveness that generally infects the American public. The entrants are reformers, composing trenchant commentaries on the state of modern literacy. If it pleasures you, you may look upon them as literary vigilantes prowling the subways of fiction.

Q. Then the contest is actually a good-natured jab at bad writing: as one journalist put it, "an exercise in humor and playful creativity, an irreverent romp across the landscape of literacy," or something.

A. Yes, each sentence is a distilled work of literary criticism, a lampoon of various species of literary malpractice.

Q. "Lampoon"! By the way, many people are curious where the term comes from. Could you enlighten them?

A. "Lampoon" is actually a compound derived from two words—"lamb" and "harpoon." A "lampoon" was a device for harpooning lambs.

Q. But you don't mean literal lambs?

A. No, "lamb" here is a ewe-phemism for anything that needs spearing, particularly of the literary persuasion.

Q. Then we might look upon this collection as a literary shish kebab.

A. A felicitous choice of words. You must have your own copy of *It Was a Dark and Stormy Night*. (Penguin Books. Available at all good bookstores.)

Q. But to return to the contest. It asks people to submit opening sentences to imaginary novels. Have you ever thought of accepting sentences from published novels?

A. Some mischief-makers have suggested this, but we have a definite policy against it. For one thing, we do not wish to give offense to the fraternity of practicing authors. After all, our ultimate commitment is to literacy and the universal improvement of mankind, so naturally we are on the side of anyone who can write books that will lure people away from their TVs. And besides, some of these writers can afford very expensive attorneys.

Q. Aren't there some non-frivolous reasons for sponsoring a contest that asks people to abuse their mother tongue? Isn't there a school of thought that relates literacy to our capacity for wordplay, which says that we can tighten our syntax and refine our imagery even as we toy with the language? Aren't there those who claim that a joyless and exclusively practical attitude toward language stifles the very affection and enthusiasm and imagination that engender great literature? Weren't Chaucer and Swift and Twain all great writers in part because they were prepared to flaunt convention and take risks?

A. So true! So true! But it doesn't hurt that the Bulwer-Lytton Contest helps draw attention to a university at a time when it is becoming prohibitively expensive to buy winning football teams.

Q. Then how much longer will you continue to stage your wretched writing contest?

A. Until people stop submitting entries or until the football team goes 11 and 0.

Q. Do you have any plans in the future for charging an entry fee to the Bulwer-Lytton Contest?

A. None. We are committed to protecting the competition from the vulgar commercialism that infects so much of American life. The Bulwer-Lytton Contest is a public service. It is enough for us knowing that we are bringing joy and release to millions of jaded, burned out, disillusioned human beings.

Q. Such selflessness is a rarity these days.

A. However, if people would like to express their gratitude and support, they could purchase copies of *It Was a Dark and Stormy Night* and *Son of "It Was a Dark and Stormy Night."* (They are inexpensive, make excellent gifts, and are printed on recycled facial tissues. Furthermore, for every ten copies you buy we will send an orphan to camp. Offer void where prohibited by the supply of orphans.)

1985 GRAND PRIZE WINNER

◇◇◇

The countdown had stalled at T minus 69 seconds when Desirée, the first female ape to go up in space, winked at me slyly and pouted her thick, rubbery lips unmistakably—the first of many such advances during what would prove to be the longest, and most memorable, space voyage of my career. —*Martha Simpson*
Glastonbury, Conn.

GRAND PANJANDRUM'S SPECIAL AWARD (1984)

◇◇◇

Awash with unfocused desire, Everett twisted the lobe of his one remaining ear and felt the presence of somebody else behind him, which caused terror to push through his nervous system like a flash flood roaring down the mid-fork of the Feather River before the completion of the Oroville Dam in 1959. —*James D. Houston*
Santa Cruz, Calif.

GRAND PANJANDRUM'S
SPECIAL AWARD (1985)

◇◇◇

Sheriff Chameleotoptor sighed with an air of weary sadness, and then turned to Doppelgutt and said, "The Senator must have really been on a bender this time—he left a party in Cleveland, Ohio, at 11:30 last night, and they found his car this morning in the smokestack of a British aircraft carrier in the Formosa Straits."

—*Robert D. Norris, Jr.*
Tulsa, Okla.

THE SUN HICCUPPED MORNING ONTO THE WEEPING LANDSCAPE

"A VAST AND BRILLIANT
PANORAMA OF
LOVE AND INTRIGUE,
PASSION AND POWER,
LUST AND AMBITION,
RAGE AND SERENITY,
FIRE AND FROST,
HOTNESS AND COLDNESS,
UH, WARMTH AND COOLNESS,
FRIENDLINESS AND
CRANKINESS . . ."

The sun hiccupped morning onto the weeping landscape as Cassandra lay on her great four-poster, one arm across her forehead, the other—soon to snap forward to pick up the alarm clock she so abhorred and hurl it through the leaded bay window of her bedroom onto the pristine green of her garden below (the sound of which would no doubt, as it did every morning, awaken the ancient butler, an old man who had worked for the family ever since its tea-planting days in far-off Sri Lanka, formerly Ceylon)—lying gracefully by her side, white and ivory-like.

—*John Weir Close*
Charlottesville, Va.

The limpid, lucid, rotund moon, resembling an oversized marshmallow, rose diffidently amongst the dark rain-pregnant clouds which scuttled across the tropic sky like cockroaches fleeing from an insect spray, whilst below, the massed palm trees, fronting the surf-crushed beach, gnashed and clashed in the thrashing wind, bending and bowing obediently to its increasingly imperious will.

—*Robert J. Hyland*
Los Angeles, Calif.

As a heedless sapling recklessly scaling love's trick ladder (which had since etched its Stygian pallor across my life's history like scar tissue), quantity, not quality, had been paramount; yet here in this unforeseen boudoir, gazing upon Noreen's candid spheroids which shone between the parted valances of her cascading hair like twin unicorns emerging from the primeval boscage, my cranium reverberated with subtle insight: all girls are not alike.

—*Chris Page*
Neenah, Wis.

The hands of the little white porcelain clock, which had sat at her bedside since she was twelve years old and wildly in love with

Baxton Heathley and which had been given to her by her aunt Martha who had since died of a mysterious ailment in Peru while reportedly seeking information on the whereabouts of the famed black diamond which had belonged to her mother and her mother before her and so on down the line until it had disappeared during a hailstorm in Kansas where she was attending a convention of Astrologers Anonymous, crept slowly. —*Dorey Hollin-Lowe*
Salinas, Calif.

It all began on a melancholy Monday, a day overshadowed by a dark, dire nimbostratus which hung over the city of Blatant Hustings like crepe over a bier, while, below, people drifted between the modern-day, glass-shot concrete obelisks of the metropolis like ghosts flitting amidst the pocked tombstones of a necropolis, their vulcanized cerecloths flapping in the mephitic urban wind, the living unconsciously playing out the roles which we, mortals that we be, must all one day assume in earnest.
—*Eugene Jones, Jr.*
Milwaukee, Wis.

With a curvaceous figure that Venus would have envied, a tanned unblemished oval face framed with lustrous thick brown hair, deep azure-blue eyes fringed with long black lashes, perfect teeth that vied for competition, and a small straight nose, Marilee had a beauty that defied description. —*Alice A. Hall*
Fort Wayne, Ind.

The November snow was thin and slushy—almost as if the angels in Heaven were brushing their teeth and dribbling toothpaste over the earth.
—*Mary Catherine Weir*
Campbell, Calif.

Nelson's doughy face came apart like a wonton stuffed by an amateur, its parts moving briskly in the boiling chicken broth of Susan's memory, its recipe resonating history, suggesting the thrust of Mongol swords into the defiant breasts of her ancestors defending the shtetl's unpenned roosters. —*Norika Sawada*
San Francisco, Calif.

The single hair on her desk ran across a peculiar configuration of wood grain outlining a perfect Sphinx—not the Babylonian type, but the well-known Egyptian one that stands (sits? lies?) marooned in the desert, except that the one which appeared on the desk had a more complete face, not eroded away, or shot away, or whatever it was that happened to the original Egyptian one that you can see on a lot of postcards and in travel magazines even today. —*Sarah A. Stranglen*
Wilmette, Ill.

Flicking back the creamy cambric of the lightly slumbering Lady Veronica's oriental gown, emblazoned with an eponymous dragon across the back and simpering succubi at each breast, Count Pendragon irritably prepared to drive the hypodermic needle and its deadly cascade of gentian poison into the blue-gray vein throbbing quietly at that wrist whose well-turned delicacy so many in their previous circle of acquaintances at court had wistfully remarked upon in their desultory postprandial conversations after breakfast. —*James Yuenger*
Chicago, Ill.

Sandra, remembering Lawrence, that spoiled only son of an indulgent and wealthy woman, past forty at his birth, which was traumatic for her and because of which she alternately pampered and abused the product of it, wishing that he were here to share

this moment of triumph with her but secretly rejoicing that she did not have to endure his tendentious assessment, which she knew would provoke an argument that would finally abrogate whatever relationship remained between them, sighed ambiguously.
—*Anne Sheppard*
Laurens, S.C.

Roberta's body, swathed in the fetid air of the third-class train compartment, was racked by amebiasis, and yet, while the train cut its path through the countryside like a scalpel transecting flesh, she felt her spirit and being perfused with radiance (that special radiance that knows no parameters), as platoons of memories marched before her eyes, wholly ravishing in their effects, their poignancy attesting to the power and mystery of this land (her recent and dear "home"), and its previously foreign peoples—massive, clotting memories, bonding Roberta extensively and for all time to this country, from which she must soon schedule egress.
—*Janet E. Johnson*
Laguna Beach, Calif.

Teetering on the brink of madness, Ravenal's brain was hanging by the fingernails to the last shreds of sanity he could muster out of the whirling maelstrom of passions that whipped and burned and threatened to drown him in an everlasting potpourri of fears, doubts, temptations, and delights that fed his soul through a sausage grinder and molded it into a palpable anguish as tortured and luminescent as rotting ham under a full moon.
—*Cecily Korell*
Arcadia, Calif.

Betty threw her head back, her light eyes sparkling like pearl onions in a particularly dry martini, her white, twig-like hands

folded on the head of the black bearskin rug, on which she was sprawled naked, her creamy buttocks rising from their black-furred surroundings like two Hostess Snowballs—the white kind, not the pink—without the encumbrance of the plastic wrapper or the annoying sticker which announces their presence but which also obscures their visibility, and laughed. —*Kevin J. Compton*
New York, N.Y.

Chauncey C. Cunningham-Clark, a concupiscent centenarian Capricorn and current comptroller of a colossal Connecticut conglomerate, was consummately chic in his cashmere coat and cardinal-colored cords as he cruised comfortably coastward in his chartreuse classic Cadillac convertible condescendingly contemplating the carefully cultivated California countryside while champion chihuahua Cochise, his cuddlesome canine companion, chewed caramel-coated corn chips and cocked his ears when "CC" cackled cheerfully in his cultured Cambridge accent, "Come Christmas, chum, you'll chomp candy canes in Carmel."
—*Bill Boyan*
Sacramento, Calif.

HER BREASTS LEAPT LIKE LIZARDS

"A LESSON IN OLD-FASHIONED STORY-TELLING (ENDLESS DESCRIPTIONS, DOZENS OF TANGENTIALLY RELATED SUB-PLOTS, MORE CHARACTERS THAN YOU CAN KEEP TRACK OF, INCESSANT AUTHORIAL INTRUSION, AND A STORY THAT SUCCEEDS IN BEING BOTH EPISODIC AND OVER-PLOTTED)."

Her breasts leapt like lizards from high cliffs as fear welled up from her chest and danced a rhumba in her throat.

—*Lucinda Ryan*
Alameda, Calif.

Her breasts rose like twin Fujiyamas, the silk of her blouse forming miniature ski runs in their folds, causing me to consider taking up cross-country skiing with a vengeance; but I chose in its stead tact as a stance as I intoned a wistful "Good evening."

—*Jonathan E. Boys*
Sargentville, Maine

Her ample bosom quivered in the night air like a whale trying to scratch its back.

—*Kevin Lauderdale*
Pasadena, Calif.

She was stacked like a fat man's plate at a one-time-through smorgasbord, so I grabbed a plate and followed in her wake.

—*Douglas B. McInnes*
Sequim, Wash.

She was like the driven snow beneath the galoshes of my lust.

—*Larry Bennett*
Chicago, Ill.

The snow fell horizontally in the driving winds that swept over the prairie and around the occasional tree, small collections of snow and dust forming in the tall grass looking remarkably like chewed Cheerios as it creeps from the corners of a baby's mouth.

—*James E. Miller*
Cherokee, Iowa

She fled before the oncoming storm, stumbling and staggering over the sharp shards of lava, shrieking, "My God, I can't stand it anymore!" as her feet began to swell like raisins plumping in hot oatmeal.
                                                        —*Helen F. Shirley*
                                                        Livermore, Calif.

Gnawing sleep from his foggy brain like a cat scratching for the last clean spot in a sandbox, he threw his feet to the cold bare floor.
                                                        —*Clinton M. Blount*
                                                        Fair Oaks, Calif.

Through the cigarette smoke neon light of the Pigalle bistro Jean-Paul noticed that although Monique's skirt was as tight as French neoclassical drama, her morals were not unlike brazen *vers libre*—unless the twelve sailors really *were* affectionate brothers who'd been overlooked when she'd earlier recalled being an only child.
                                                        —*John Balkwill*
                                                        Hampton, Va.

Like a freshly cracked egg with its yolk hanging desperately to its white precious milliseconds before breaking free and slithering with a thud to its designated container, I clung to the cliff in fear.
                                                        —*J. P. Van Landingham, Jr.*
                                                        Mount Pleasant, S.C.

The great orange tennis ball of the sun had scarcely been batted over the net of the horizon by some cosmic John McEnroe, when the lambent violet eyes of Radclyffe Holloware, the lovely twenty-six-year-old cat litter tycoon, opened to greet this most important day—the day that would make or break Cat's Head, the day when six months of careful planning might at last culminate in what she so passionately desired, the takeover of her one

remaining rival in the rough-and-tumble world of cat sanitation, Kitty-Loo—and immediately leaping from between her white-Zinfandel-colored sheets, she cast aside her tastefully feminine gown of brie-colored chiffon to begin her grueling aerobics workout which would, she hoped, hone the edges of her Cuisinart-blade mind so that nothing could distract her from her purpose, not even the dark hypnotic eyes of Kitty-Loo's ruggedly handsome president, Buster Bullgrass.
—*Geraldine Daesch*
Redwood City, Calif.

The tire swing undulated in the shade of the old oak tree like an upside-down lollipop on a pendulum, while three little boys, tanned from their summer frolicking, clung to the swing like flies trapped on an open-faced honey sandwich.
—*Niels Leppert-Köhler*
Providence, R.I.

As hot thunder rolled like labor pains from a black, rain-pregnant sky, and wind-whipped Gulf waters broke along the smooth white leg of beach, Stella's foot slipped alternately between the accelerator and brake of her baby-blue hatchback as she sped along the dark Coast road which would wind like an umbilical cord, deep into the center of the swamp, where, at the pinkish blush of dawn, Stanley would be expecting her.
—*C. W. Kelly*
South Pasadena, Calif.

Dawn laid one bright claw across the sky, and the bloated orange body of the sun crab, like a rounded *Niña, Pinta,* or *Santa Maria* conquering the curvature of the earth, elbowed its way over the horizon.
—*Ann Adams*
Oak Harbor, Wash.

Ah, sweet misery! like the taste of a hundred rotten apples, a thousand anchovies with extra salt, ten thousand glasses of sour milk, a hundred thousand pints of that chalky stuff they make you drink before taking your X-ray. —*Robert Alan Rabinowitz*
Tempe, Ariz.

As Roland slithered from a sly fox-trot into a torrid fandango, Melanie felt herself collapsing in his arms like meringue, or maybe like a slightly warmed raspberry sauce, or no, she de-cided—definitely like a pêche flambée, but of course lit up on all the edges.   —*Sarah Remington*
Dublin, Calif.

THE JUNGLE DRUMS THROBBED WILDLY

"A KNUCKLE-WHITENING,
BREATH-TAKING,
HEART-GRABBING,
STOMACH-CHURNING,
BUN-CLENCHING
PAGE-TURNER
THAT WILL LEAVE
YOU GASPING FOR RELIEF."

The jungle drums throbbed wildly in the distance, warning him away with a brief but dire message: "The broccoli casserole is burnt!"
—*Pat Walker*
Garden Grove, Calif.

Phillips jumped from the hovering helicopter into the drift, which had the consistency of cream cheese, and, weighted down by his gear, sank quickly like a suppository into the bowels of the icy tundra while the snow swirled around him as if a million feathers from ripped pillows had been tossed and slammed against his head during some giant, crazy, Jovian pillow fight.
—*Jeff Parmer*
Fargo, N.D.

Glory tucked the remains of the unfortunate Nigel under her arm as she squinted into the sun, scanning the horizon for the hyenas, the cannibals, and the rapacious Nazis she knew lay between her and the ivory idol of the Mother Goddess, and she began setting one determined foot in front of the other, impervious to the hot sand that seared the soles of her woman-flesh.
—*Sherry Eslick Buettgenbach*
Wichita, Kans.

"Cultural Anthropology!" he snorted sardonically, standing in the clearing in the rain forest, a soggy Carlton between his lips, a fleet of insects orbiting the flame of his disposable lighter, a poison dart dangling impotently from the collar of his safari jacket, and a case of jock itch that would have made a three-toed sloth mean.
—*Ed Tootill*
Philadelphia, Pa.

The caravan was not moving and Manfred Bellview, a six-foot two-inch British ex-juggler, by trade, was not a waiter by nature

(although at 16, during one hot summer, he had bussed some tables in his American Aunt Ruby's ramshackle café in Quakenbush, New Jersey), so he pushed past the verdant Congolese jungle and with a swipe of his hand knocked three loud and discourteous pit vipers from his safari-hat, then edged to the front of the party, where he discovered precisely what had been slowing its progress—his wife (Nellie Bly), his best friend (Herman Wrinspot), and his pet chimpanzee (Becky) were locked in what can be best described as a deep triangular kiss, though the chimp withdrew on a periodic basis to chew a banana which it held in its free hand.
　　　　　　　　　　　　　　　　　　　—*S. Bradley Sayre*
　　　　　　　　　　　　　　　　　　　　Santa Barbara, Calif.

Straining against the thick lianas that bound him to the altar of Godok-Mokol and wincing as an army ant bit yet another nickel-sized chunk out of his thigh, Derek eyed the obsidian blade poised over his heart, soon to slice that organ out beating into the hands of a kohl-eyed priestess, and fervently prayed that Chuckie the gorilla would grab the right banana—the one with the vial of nitro secreted inside.
　　　　　　　　　　　　　　　　　　　—*Rodney G. Webre*
　　　　　　　　　　　　　　　　　　　　Austin, Tex.

The Morro Bay Tour Boat whistle, hooting an earsplitting hysterical signal, frantically called for help as each new wave of the rising tide dashed the boat's length ever harder against the stone breakwater, smashing wider the gaping hole through which one hundred thirty-two almost survivors bounced along the foam in bright orange life vests, looking for all the world like a flotilla of odd water bugs adventuring outside the harbor.
　　　　　　　　　　　　　　　　　　　—*Velda Markham*
　　　　　　　　　　　　　　　　　　　　Riverdale, Calif.

She struggled to climb the rocky bank, and to be free of the heavy, clinging mud that crushed me, pushed the air from my lungs, held me pinioned like a vise, as sucking sounds of the mud reluctantly releasing her heels mocked a dirge—perhaps my last, I shuddered—as she stripped off her pantyhose, flung me a foot, and began to crawl slowly toward the trees with the leg stretching until it twanged like a high-tension wire and she disappeared from sight.

—*Dorothy J. Shannon*
Ramona, Calif.

Wilkens, the tall muscular fisherman, shielded himself with his pantyhose by tugging it up and over his head and holding it there while the arrows shot by the Eskimo sailors bounced mercifully off him and didn't hurt him either because apparently they could not pierce the fine knit fabric, especially the "control top."

—*Tom Dempsey*
Cambridge, Mass.

Champ Hensley's laugh was harsh and cruel as he pointed off the bow of his smuggling trawler and fiercely spat the world "sharkbait" at his terrified captive, but little had he reckoned that her golden tresses and angelic green eyes would start an avalanche of life-changing passion somewhere deep inside his barrel chest, an avalanche caused when a chunk of his stone heart, like a boulder dislodging from a cliff face, broke away and plummeted into the dark gorge of his stomach.

—*Larry Isitt*
Coeur D'Alene, Idaho

Harvey tightened the belt of his trench coat, eyed the whirring prop of the ceiling fan, settled deeper into the cobra-backed chair situated among the dusty palms in the ratty Mediterranean hotel lobby, and then spat out the large swig of his drink he had just taken when it proved that the sliver of ice sliding across his tongue had legs.
—*Dana Elaine Carr*
Shawnee, Kans.

Red Joppits smacked the fully-loaded clip of 9mm ammo hard into the black steel butt of the Beretta, clenching his jaw tightly, eyes blazing hard like new-frozen ice as he flipped back the heavy cocking slide to thrust a copper-jacketed slug into the hungry chamber of his battle-proven semi-automatic firing piece; then "Jesus!" he gasped, as he realized the skin of one of his fingers was trapped under the sharp metal sliding rail of the useless hunk of scrap iron.
—*David H. Patterson*
Bartlesville, Okla.

"Over the top be damned!" snorted Sergeant York as he took careful aim at his seldom-needed little toe, and coincidentally at his post-retirement hopes of peddling fake plaster-of-Paris impressions of prominent ballet dancers' feet at county fairs.
—*Robert F. Gannon*
Chino, Calif.

Wisteria had not the foggiest notion why she had been abducted in the dead of night by masked ruffians, trussed feet and hands, and brought to this hovel in the depths of the forest, but her legs and arms had long since become numb to beyond feeling any pain; her throat dry beyond crying out for help which would never arrive anyway; and her eyes bemused as they watched the large scorpion make its slow, investigatory journey up her long skirt and across her lap; while what remained of her reason reached back, grasping fleetingly onto the long-forgotten nursery rhyme as she giggled faintly and ran light-heartedly after little Miss Muffet down the path to merciful oblivion.

—*Elaine Huegel*
Green Bay, Wis.

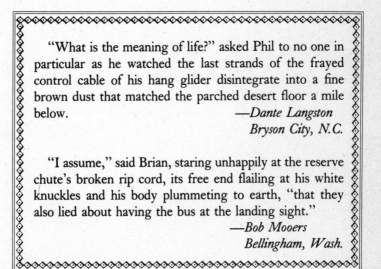

"What is the meaning of life?" asked Phil to no one in particular as he watched the last strands of the frayed control cable of his hang glider disintegrate into a fine brown dust that matched the parched desert floor a mile below. —*Dante Langston*
Bryson City, N.C.

"I assume," said Brian, staring unhappily at the reserve chute's broken rip cord, its free end flailing at his white knuckles and his body plummeting to earth, "that they also lied about having the bus at the landing sight."
—*Bob Mooers*
Bellingham, Wash.

"CALLING
ALL
BUNNIES!"

"JANEY THOUGHT
THIS WOULD
BE HER DUMBEST,
BORINGEST
SUMMER EVER.
THEN SHE MET
RAOUL!"

"Calling all bunnies!" shouted Randy the Happy Wizard as he shook his carrot out the window of his jolly house in Old Mr. Oak on the edge of the Peppermint Stick Garden.

—*Bill Dignin*
San Mateo, Calif.

In today's lesson, boys and girls (from our super-secret book of things we don't always tell our mommies and daddies), we are going to learn about all the wonderful, fun things you can make with a combination of feather dusters, English peas, and your next-door neighbor's kitty cat. —*Carol Ann Webb*
Atlanta, Ga.

Once there were five children whose names were Nigel, Agatha, Ian, Eudora, and Bruce, and this is the story about some perfectly splendid things that happened to them when they went away to live with Professor Edmund, a dear chap, who lived in a large house full of unexpected places with several servants named Mildred, Betty, Jeeves, and Brewster, but they do not have much to do with the story.

(from *The Lynx, the Wizard, and the Chifforobe*)
—*Gail Cain*
San Francisco, Calif.

"Beep! Beep!" barked Bones the Mechanical Dog as he ran round and round the Christmas tree, waking the sleepy-eyed toys beneath its sparkling boughs, warning everyone about the red-suited, red-booted, hirsute stranger stuck fast in the flue of their chimney. —*Shirley Climo*
Los Altos, Calif.

Itsey-Bitsey (who looked suspiciously like a small, gray, fuzzy-furry kitten) was trying and trying to figure out how she could

persuade her mother (who looked suspiciously like a large, white, fuzzy-furry *cat* but was the most beautiful creature Itsey-Bitsey had ever seen) to let her go out and play in the deep, green forest that was so full of wonderful sounds and sights and smells that it positively made her whiskers quiver! —*Dena Leathem*
Parks, Ariz.

"Crap!" spat Timmy through clenched teeth, "ain't no way these chicks is gonna come across before my mom gets home unless we can get 'em stoned-out real fast, and that up-tight witch has hid the coke so good this time even Sissy can't find it, and she could find gravy in a cesspool."
(From #13 in the series Contemporary Fiction for Youngsters Who Hate to Read) —*Cecily Korell*
Arcadia, Calif.

In a comfortable cottage on the hill (furnished mostly with Victorian oddments and endments) there lived a small ordinary, everyday babbit with no magical powers at all except the kind that allowed him to slay slimy dragons, massacre regiments of goblins, and save helpless villagers from power-mad sorcerers; mostly, though, he liked to stay at home and swill tea.
—*Gail Cain*
San Francisco, Calif.

Old Poppa Bear and Aloysius Bear and Cuthbert Bear and Little Baby Bear all lived together in Bear Forest, a tiny wee cottage in a thicket by the sea, and gave psychic readings, did tarot, and conned the natives as best they could.
—*D. C. Cameron*
South Laguna, Calif.

Once upon a time there was a little boy—just like you!—named Jeff, and he lived in a yellow house with a big yard, along with his mother and father and sister and brother and his bunny rabbit (until it got loose and Mr. Koberly's dog ate it) and his goldfish (that his brother flushed down the toilet one day when he got mad at Jeff) and his puppy, Squitters, that ran in front of a car just a few weeks after Jeff's mom had to go to the hospital for an operation (only the operation didn't work, and Jeff's mommy went to Heaven); but before Jeff got leukemia and died, he and his puppy had this exciting adventure . . . —*Cynthia Conyers*
Aguanaga, Calif.

Jason walked along the street, feeling the wad of money in his faded blue Levi's, and every time he felt it rub in his pocket up against his thigh he smiled; but in the back of his mind Jason wondered if his mother would be as happy as he was that he had sold Petey, his little brother, to the gypsies passing through town.
—*Richard W. Brown*
Scottville, Mich.

As the golden rays of afternoon deepened to evening, a tender, flaxen-haired child sat at the window, two gin-scented tears trickling down her cheeks as she—with such dread and fear and trembling that it would make your socks quite wet to ponder it—awaited the arrival of the two men costumed in black armbands and grey weasel furs, who the previous evening had intruded on her happy life with their terrible words: "Dear, innocent child, prepare yourself to depart with us very soon, for your dear mother's unfortunate accident with the lace and the coffee grounds have left you an orphan, and now the shuttlecocks and the limbs and the groaning spiders of the workhouse await you."
—*Jan Bender*
Los Angeles, Calif.

LYTTONY I

"FROM THE PRINCE OF PEACE
ROCK CONCERT TO THE 'PILL,
SNIFF, AND SWIG FARM' AND
THE COEDS AT MEDUSA
COLLEGE"

It was at the Prince of Peace rock concert that a nefarious culprit must have surreptitiously drugged my diet cola (although I preferred the clear, effervescent taste of 7-Up, but that the Orange Bowl vendor asserted he was out of) as it was passed hand by hand down the line of devout music lovers, and I awakened to find myself sans clothing on this satin-sheeted water bed and wondered pensively, as was my habit, whether Mother Superior would accept my explanation for being tardy to vespers.

—*Marilyn S. Funderburk*
Fort Lauderdale, Fla.

In prelude to her daily vigil Sister Autorella flattened herself against the outer wall of the small, sixteenth-century chapel, moved furtively toward the carved wooden doors, and peered cautiously inside, wondering, as also was her habit, if she'd be able to complete at least two stations of the cross before the first of the cathedral tours exploded the solitude so vital for her meditations.

—*T. Holt Sutton*
Pebble Beach, Calif.

The thick brown air assaulted her eyes and lungs and the cacophony of commute-hour horns drowned out the cathedral bells, and Sister Innocentia surveyed the gridlock, shifted her battered valise to the other shoulder, nimbly sidestepped an ancient black Plymouth that cut across the broad sidewalk, accurately aimed one scuffed oxford at the groin of the largest of the unkempt urchins attempting to separate her from her handbag (thereby scattering the others momentarily), and wondered for the hundredth time since the bus for Vera Cruz deposited her on the Paseo de la Reforma an hour earlier whether God had taken leave of his senses, whether she had committed some inadvertent (but ob-

viously insignificant) sin, and what the angel in her dream could possibly have had in mind.   —*Denis W. Wade*
San Francisco, Calif.

"Suck hot lead, Yankee Schweine!" bellowed Sister Regina as she flung aside the front of her habit to reveal a somewhat antiquated but still quite deadly Schmeisser automatic, and the very last things Bobrowski and the Sarge saw—with an almost preternatural clarity—were the twin black SS lightning bolts tattooed on the satiny white skin of her left inner thigh, just above the top of her spiked-heel boot; and Sarge mouthed the words, "I guess Rocco was right about her after all," but he gagged on the warm salty blood rushing like a geyser up his throat, and only a low gurgling hiss emerged from his mouth before his newly perforated back slapped the rain-slicked flagstones of the little piazza, even as the colossal silver intergalactic cruiser, its inboard running lights flickering hypnotically, settled to an eerily silent landing behind the bombed-out rectory.   —*Karl M. Petruso*
Brookline, Mass.

The priest cradled an ornate crucifix in his left arm while he stood watching her thrashing about on the violently rocking bed, a thin stream of ectoplasm seeping from her nose, her preternaturally harsh voice spewing curses and filth in several languages into the putrid air—and when he thought of the great sport of the next few hours, he laughed till he wept.   —*Harry De Puy*
Rochester, N.Y.

"The toilet's stopped up again!" screeched Esmeralda Fnark in a voice that had failed to endear her to over fifteen men in the past three years.   —*Michael K. Young*
Randallstown, Md.

The coeds at Medusa College seemed very bright, but Rusty did not find their appearances quite so pleasing; indeed he mistook one of the dorms for a classic Gothic cathedral until he got closer and saw that what he had at first taken to be gargoyles were really just some of the girls leaning out of the third-floor windows.

—*Robert D. Norris, Jr.*
Tulsa, Okla.

"What is death?" Sheena mused prettily, pink finger twisting a fat, golden curl, pearly brow furrowed in spiderweb lines, emerald eyes glazed in concentration, and rosebud lips pursed sweetly in thought—surely a monumental question to be answered by this winsome slip of a girl who had never had to ponder anything weightier than "What color eyeshadow should I wear tonight with my silver lamé gown sewn all over with tiny seed pearls—true blue or gallant green?"

—*Rose B. Koniar*
St. Francis, Wis.

Susan, barefoot, and carrying her wardrobe in a pillow slip, would have made good her escape from the "Pill, Sniff, and Swig Farm" by sprinting through the cow pasture to I-51 to flag the New Orleans–bound bus, had the night watchman not heard her ejaculate in a loathing and agonized voice, "I've had to listen to this stuff all of my 16 years, but never was it between my toes and freedom before!"

—*H. Curtis Flowers*
Jackson, Miss.

There was only one time in my life when I was happy to find a hair in my milk.

—*Anita Locke*
Kensington, Md.

Gregor Samsa awoke one morning and found that he had not turned into a hideous giant insect, and he was determined to mop

up all the parking lots in downtown Prague with the face of this Kafka fellow who had been spreading this wild story about him through the neighborhood.   —*Kevin D. Kelley*
Piedmont, Calif.

Her gray hair pinned back in a tight bun, Miss Aunt B. (for that's what everybody in Demopolis called her) straightened up from the stark and lovely rack of distinctive green and orange Penguin Classics she was stocking and, winking at the signed photographs of Faulkner and Capote which flanked the framed first dollar bill The Haunted Bookshoppe had taken in, turned to the overweight matron in cerise who was holding a clothbound copy of Jacqueline Susann's *Once Is Not Enough* and replied, "It's about the second coming of Christ!"   —*Rosa Crucial*
Fairhope, Ala.

NEVER FREEZE BRIE!

"SHE WAS A
SAVAGE BEAUTY
—WILD, UNTAMED
(OR AT LEAST
NOT HOUSE-BROKEN
YET)."

Sszzzz! Lard billowed into a black cloud as fourteen-year-old Bambi began to fry her first meal for hunky Matt, her husband of three days, her sex-fevered brain blocking out all she had learned in her gourmet cooking class except the peremptory warning: "Never freeze brie!"
—*F. Charles Woodruff*
Redwood City, Calif.

Vanessa's vision of happiness was close to being marred by Winston's unfortunate preference for canned dog food rather than for her meat loaf, the recipe for which she had striven so long to perfect, although it should be noted that he did go in for the better brands and not that cheap stuff.
—*Hurley Daughtrey*
Stone Mountain, Ga.

As Henry removed the soiled nylon stocking from his slice of lemon pie (the hosiery having been ingeniously sculpted atop the pastry's filling to form an utterly convincing, one might even say appetizing, meringue topping), he realized the day was drawing near when he would need to arrange a seemingly unarranged fatal accident to befall his somewhat less than epicurean wife, and thus end these culinary nightmares forever—in the meantime he would stock up on Sara Lee's.
—*Rick Martin*
Tulsa, Okla.

Jack was going to be there in five minutes for dinner when Jill discovered she had baked her lipstick in the lasagne.
—*Mollie Sluss*
Winnetka, Ill.

On this fifth morning of Juby's new but still unconsummated marriage, the scrambled eggs, looking like cow paddies dropped

from a disgruntled bovine with peptic ulcers in three of her four stomachs, lay on his plate like an ominous forecast of the day yet to be weathered.
—*Edward L. Recod*
Sacramento, Calif.

Prudence watched, giddy with repulsion, as Purvis—her husband of seventeen hours and eleven minutes—labored over his obscene repast, ladling spoonfuls of glutinous marmalade over the kippered herrings that lay singed and melancholy on their beds of soggy rice, oblivious to the fact that she was still in possession of her prized and burdensome maidenhead—and knew that at the preordained moment she must, out of duty, stab him with the butter knife.
—*Anneke Dubash*
Ottawa, Ontario

Roland blinked, then blinked again as he looked around the smoke-filled room to see Elsa at the piano, her hair a pile of blond sauerkraut bobbing in time with the music she played, Edgar watching her with admiring black olive eyes above a dill pickle nose while Milton, his complexion like tapioca pudding, danced with the gold lamé sausage that was Alice, and he knew it was time either to stop drinking martinis or to quit his job at the deli.
—*Nancy C. Swoboda*
Omaha, Nebr.

The fiery wind of the raging tempest buffeted its bitter tirade on the little ship, and Gwendolyn, staggering blindly about the deck, felt her already agitated stomach slosh queasily to and fro, while fathoms below its petulant surface, the hearty life-spawning Pacific teemed with the succulent coral-pink shrimp that Gwen was so fond of suspending in her world-famous raspberry cream cheese

cheese gelatin mold, three-time winner of the annual Say-It-with-Salad Savory Slice-Off.
—*Carrie Sogg*
Los Gatos, Calif.

She would barely recover from one wave of nausea before the next came crashing over her, leaving her little of her dignity and none of her lunch.
—*Carolyn King Fitzgerald*
Merritt Island, Fla.

Her always delicate stomach heaving, copper-haired, emerald-eyed Jessamyn Whitehurst grasped the spray-slimed rail of the *Fairhope of Berwick-upon-Tweed* and gave herself, and the last hour's salt-pork chowder, up to the churning maelstrom of the storm-lashed channel.
—*Lorrie Farrelly*
Orange, Calif.

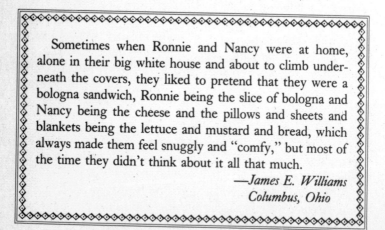

Sometimes when Ronnie and Nancy were at home, alone in their big white house and about to climb underneath the covers, they liked to pretend that they were a bologna sandwich, Ronnie being the slice of bologna and Nancy being the cheese and the pillows and sheets and blankets being the lettuce and mustard and bread, which always made them feel snuggly and "comfy," but most of the time they didn't think about it all that much.
—*James E. Williams*
Columbus, Ohio

IN DUBIOUS TASTE

"A BOOK SO BOLD,
SO DARING, SO TOTALLY
OUTRAGEOUS THAT
NO ONE ELSE
WOULD PUBLISH IT
—AND NEITHER WOULD
WE, SO WE
PUBLISHED THIS ONE
INSTEAD."

As if on cue, the dark clouds began spitting at passersby, not the warm watery spit that mistakenly passes one's lips while speaking, or a little stream emitted by a playful saliva gland, but the thick, heavy spittle that is brought up dark, humid bronchial tubes, a pulsating esophagus, and spewed forth by dirty-mouthed boys trying to be men. —*Michele M. Ruby*
Fresno, Calif.

It was to one of the danker atolls in the Pacific (piña coladas and hula dancing notwithstanding—such islands, you will agree, have humid and mysterious reputations), where a colony of lepers flourished like canker sores in the mouths of the caves which pockmarked the island's shore, that Wendy was sent to bring The Word, for it was feared that should this petri dish of decaying culture be left unattended those stricken with the dread disease would rot in hell as surely as they were on earth.
—*Melissa M. McCarter*
Seattle, Wash.

As she looked down at the battered and bloodied body before her, Grace felt a little disappointed in herself for having so brutally beaten Bobby Meyer to death, but even after thirty-two years of teaching, the one thing she had never quite learned to tolerate was a student who picked his nose and then ate it.
—*Rose Mary Gergick*
Tonganoxie, Kans.

Bethune knew his chances with Dimpled Elaine had diminished considerably the moment whatever it was fell from his nostril, uncurled, and scooted away. —*Craig Marshall Smith*
Aurora, Colo.

"My dearest Beowulf, you cannot tell me," cried Lorelei gaily, as she plunged her slim white arm oxter-deep into the Guernsey's rectum, "that the thrill of bringing relief to these poor, suffering animals does not transcend that felt by the chemist who has just devised a new, improved underarm deodorant."

—*Barrie Collins*
La Salle, Quebec

In the nightmare dead of winter, skirting a smog-bound metropolis, the sluggish river moved silent and odious beneath the rampant gray arc of a sky, carrying with it the frozen, bloated remains of those reckless derelicts who leaned too far forward to puke.

—*Jaime Rush*
Anchorage, Alaska

Romano stomped on the grapes with furious abandon, knowing in the depth of his being that he was making a major contribution toward the laying down of a fine vintage wine, and that he was also well on his way toward permanently curing his bunions and chilblains—but would it solve the nagging problem of his weak kidneys?

—*Lee DiAngelo*
St. Petersburg, Fla.

Maurice Twittlecock III hastily adjourned the board-of-directors meeting in time for the scraping of chairs and shuffling of wing-tip-clad feet to amply muffle the escaping essence of his cheesy-bean burrito.

—*Wanda Henson*
Sausalito, Calif.

The hot, humid air was like a blanket, a heavy, damp blanket, and Paul Conklin hated blankets, heavy, damp blankets, more than anything else in the world—"except fat women," thought

Paul, "fat, sweaty women, who cover a man like a heavy, damp blanket."

—*W. H. Owens*
Mesa, Ariz.

"The shame of syphilis," sniggered the pathologist, all the while toying with his scalpel, "is that nobody succumbs to it anymore."

—*Dr. Charles C. Mehegan*
Erie, Pa.

Butterworth sang bad opera while Natalie's shapely legs were taking forever to be eaten away—"O Freedom Mio! O Freedom Mio!" he was ranting crazily to a lone fly who had engorged himself on the bloody trail from the verandah and retired to the rim of the tub—when a strangely fluorescent hand became airborne above the bubble bath of acid, pointed familiarly at Butterworth's frozen face with a long-nailed finger still glossed with impervious red polish, and then slapped the torporous insect into a little puddle of guts.

—*C. Thomas Markham*
Eastsound, Wash.

Sally smacked her blood-red lips as the portly waitress served her the kiwi torte, and not a minute too soon did she do this, since Sally needed to pull up her too-tight panty hose which were slowly creeping down her sumptuous derrière.

—*Juanita Rusev*
San Francisco, Calif.

As the flames lapped at the logs like his loyal labrador Laddie licking his loins, Desmond lifted the luscious licorice-laced liqueur to his lips, laughed out loud while his libido longed for the licentious librarian, Lucille, lamented over his life—a struggle between love and lust—and then looked lackadaisically at Laddie,

who was lifting his leg to let loose a liberal line of lucent lemon liquid on the divan.
—*James E. Williams*
Columbus, Ohio

No one but a myopic hydrocephalic would have considered Angela attractive, but it was her good fortune that Lloyd was a myopic hydrocephalic.
—*David L. Shumway*
Algona, Iowa

Ten Ton Tillie (it was only a nickname of course, although many a sensitive swain might well have begged to dispute that, for she had mashed Matthew in his time; she had flattened Frank; Horace had been crushed as by an Alpine avalanche; and nothing was left of Maurice but a thin, green line, like the trail left by an escargot, as the French call them—for it takes a Frog to make a delicacy of slime encased in a shell) tucked into another tantalizing, tempting tidbit and sighed, "Is there nothing in life but *déjà vu?*"
—*Eve Holmquist*
Saratoga, Calif.

There is no truth in the rumor that I am senile—forgetful surely, incontinent often, slovenly at the best of times—but control of the Blitzerman Foundation will remain in these liver-spotted hands until the call goes out to the Neptune Society.
—*Keith Wadsworth*
Los Altos Hills, Calif.

The rather well-nourished buxomly matron waddled through the pulsating pedestrian traffic of Hong Kong, pensively meditating on the problems of being a big-breasted, broad-butted, broad broad abroad.
—*Michael A. O'Neill*
Rohnert Park, Calif.

A SUBTLE BREEZE TEASED THE MAINSAILS

"A GRIPPING NOVEL THAT WILL
LEAVE YOU FEELING WRUNG
OUT—OR IS IT A
WRINGING NOVEL THAT WILL
LEAVE YOU FEELING
GROPED OUT?—
WELL, ANYWAY . . ."

A subtle breeze teased the mainsails as Lady Brestin, bedizened in pink and green with matching pumps and parasol and appearing on the poop deck for the first time since her abduction, wondered both whether all pirates were as perverse as this godless gang and if they would ever return any of her pantaloons— not that she would ever let them touch her pale skin after those riffraff had worn them, of course. —*Dave Page*
Minneapolis, Minn.

"Aye, and now ye scum be pirates and outlaws of the seven seas," roared the feared Cap'n Redbeard, "and the only laws ye'll follow, and live, are mine—ye'll pillage, rape, and murder without mercy when'er I tells ye, and ye'll go potty over the starb'rd rail or get ninety tastes of me whip. —*Joseph Peter Myers*
Riverside, Calif.

Anthony Bollard had been sent to sea by his father at age six on HMS *Perisher,* and in his thirty-four years since had learned much of His Majesty's navy but little of women, so that he was now in considerable confusion at the sunlit garden party with this dazzling creature before him in the crinoline hoop skirt, which would make a perfect cover for the anchor windlass, but which she would probably be reluctant to give up.—*John E. Rogers*
Washington, D.C.

The lovely Lenore pranced precariously in her petticoats along the widow's walk, waving her tatted kerchief, while from afar Captain Silverthorn's steel-gray eye remained transfixed to the glass as he espied the vision from the bow of the schooner, when suddenly the cruel hand of Fate, in the form of a brisk nor'easterly, swept under Lenore's voluminous skirts and sent her sailing off her perch (this Silverthorn watched in impotent horror, but

was roused from despair at the thought of the young Nubian housed in his cabin below).
—*Barbara Hegdal*
Rocklin, Calif.

Anything for a joke, grumbled the ship's doctor, as he swiftly stitched the little priestess (now in deep alpha) into the fish belly with stout twine; whereupon, Captain Jolly—after a practice kick to tease the sharks—dispatched the wench with such force that "HOLY MACKEREL!!" sprang spontaneously from every throat.
—*Jean Farmer*
Bloomington, Ind.

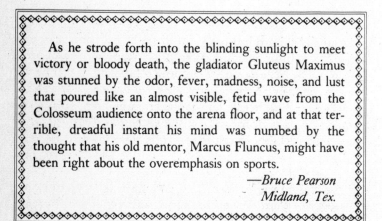

As he strode forth into the blinding sunlight to meet victory or bloody death, the gladiator Gluteus Maximus was stunned by the odor, fever, madness, noise, and lust that poured like an almost visible, fetid wave from the Colosseum audience onto the arena floor, and at that terrible, dreadful instant his mind was numbed by the thought that his old mentor, Marcus Fluncus, might have been right about the overemphasis on sports.
—*Bruce Pearson*
Midland, Tex.

Roland Roadrunner, stoutly resolving to storm the stronghold of Attila the Lout guarded by his snarling mutt in order to rescue his beautiful, innocent young daughter, Rhonda, who had insisted that she could take care of herself, courageously approached the forbidden door and, extending his hand, called to the vicious canine sentinel, "Here doggie, good doggie!" only to stand shocked and disbelieving on hearing issue from inside the richly draped sanctum a feminine voice that sounded suspiciously like Rhonda's purring, "Yes, Att honey, emeralds are nice, but I like ice."

—*Doris B. Williams*
Tulsa, Okla.

The gallant hussar astride his wind-blown steed with raised, bloody saber in hand closed ever faster to the mouth of the rebel cannon, where he saw to his horror the blond, voluptuous Olivia slowly lower the fire to the touchhole, and he knew he had once again been badly cuckolded. —*M. J. Loffler*
Fort Bragg, Calif.

Sleek she was, as velvet night, like a backdrop for the stars of her eyes, and her power was great as her beauty, the beauty of all who had borne the proud name of Princess Tot Al Wo'm An before her and who would bear it after her, after she bore those who would bear the pride of the name she bore, whom she would bear as proudly as she bared her beauty to the bore who bared his love before her barely concealed boredom.

—*Jaye Moretz*
Pleasant Hill, Calif.

Ripping the third bodice from Belinda's hot, palpitating body, Lord Trewithit realized that he had also removed four camisoles, six petticoats, two corsets, and five pairs of pantaloons so far and

there still seemed a lot of linen ahead, and with a cry of passion he demanded, "Good God, woman, are you nothing but skivvies?"
—*Gretchen S. Ellis*
Houston, Tex.

In a towering rage, the tall, tousled, bearded man shook his short, plump wife viciously, snarled at the child cowering in a corner, kicked the unoffending dog, threw pen after pen into the fire, glared all around, separated and lifted the tails of his long alpaca coat, settled into a chair—and only then did the passionate words begin to flow smoothly across the heretofore immaculate page: "Four score and seven years ago . . ." —*Harry De Puy*
Rochester, N.Y.

In the sunny summer days that preceded the outbreak of the Great War (or World War I, as it is now so inadequately known), a false but peaceful calm spread over most of Europe: emperors ruled, queens reigned, great ladies played, teacups clattered, and simple folk worked from dawn to dusk, as was right.
—*Donald C. Cameron*
South Laguna, Calif.

AS FARMER SYMCZYK AND FAMILY ASCENDED INTO HEAVEN

"A BLOCKBUSTER,
A TOWERING—NO,
MORE THAN THAT,
AN OVERTOWERING
NOVEL THAT HAS ALL
THE INGREDIENTS
(WELL, SOME OF THEM)
OF GREAT FICTION."

The first rays of the morning sun cast crisp catwalks through the gentle and fragrant pine grove where the smoldering fire circle was the only evidence of the cheese festival, complete with miniaturized cows, that had taken place there the evening before and had concluded with the actual ascension of Farmer Symczyk and family into Heaven or someplace up beyond the clouds, and the last that the other revelers saw of them was Jimmy, the littlest Symczyk, waving his fluorescent "A-Team" lunch box with the picture of Mr. T eating a car on it at them from about 10,000 feet up.   —*Tom Dempsey*
Cambridge, Mass.

The slight pressure between his eyes puzzled Tyler since the telltale tinkle had told him that his pince-nez had tumbled during their tustle; the conundrum was clarified when, upon opening his glazed eyes, he discovered the prehensile tip of Freita Mannlicher's marvelous gelatinous tongue—the remainder of which snaked up his shirt before reemerging out his collar—gently grasping the bridge of his nose.   —*Raphael X. Reichert*
Fresno, Calif.

When Guinevere heard Beauregard clattering his teeth in semblance of a rattlesnake she gnashed her own, forgetting momentarily the English walnut she was holding within her choppers, and swooned, not exactly frothing at the mouth but bleeding profusely, enough indeed to require the services of an advanced technician.   —*Natalie Henderson*
Laguna Niguel, Calif.

Her eyes were certainly the same—two small whole-wheat doughnuts, the centers plugged with fudge, and below them, in seeming perpetuity, welling tears akin to the clear liquid found

around the lip of a mayonnaise jar—as Roy-Glenn, entering her life again, this time as a quadrant coordinator for the Red Cross, informed Daisy that everything she'd owned had been sucked into Omaha.
                                        —*Wayne Shannon*
                                        San Francisco, Calif.

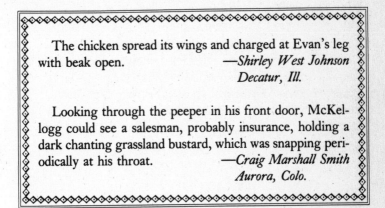

The chicken spread its wings and charged at Evan's leg with beak open.   —*Shirley West Johnson*
                                        Decatur, Ill.

Looking through the peeper in his front door, McKellogg could see a salesman, probably insurance, holding a dark chanting grassland bustard, which was snapping periodically at his throat.   —*Craig Marshall Smith*
                                        Aurora, Colo.

How could Nigel have possibly perceived that at the precise moment he was lighting his Bunsen in the lab at the university, Enid Carp, his wife of forty-two years, and a matron at the State Penitentiary for Tawdry Women, was conducting an unauthorized body cavity search for contraband cosmetics?
                                        —*Peggy Baranowski*
                                        Fremont, Calif.

Filbert's beanie propeller, caught in a sudden updraft in the Bank of America Plaza, snatched him off his delivery bike and whirled him skyward, plunking him down onto Transamerica's

lofty spire, where now he is slowly spinning in the wind at a constant fifteen revolutions per minute. —*William D. Cox*
San Francisco, Calif.

Her hunger for him seemed insatiable and as the fluffy black curtain of unconsciousness slowly descended he was only partly aware of the incredibly large slice of white bread that covered him. —*Al Keuter*
Santa Cruz, Calif.

The Dwarf had seemed mild-mannered enough at first, but as she strained against the rusty iron bracelets which held her fast to the ancient stones, her shapely bosom heaving, Slobodanka suspected that perhaps she had angered him by carelessly whistling "Short People" as they gingerly made love on the rough boards which were the dusty floor of the Doctor's laboratory.

—*T. O'Carroll*
Lawrence, Mich.

With six-guns blazing she fought her way through the crowded saloon, never stopping to worry about where she'd left her clothes or the man in the rabbit suit she'd just left upstairs.
—*Jan Butchart*
Waukesha, Wis.

Only the brave full moon and the wispy little clouds skimming across the sky saw what happened in the burial ground fenced off from the sanctified churchyard that night, for the stars blinked and turned away, and the trees shuddered their leaves and whispered to each other that they must not look at the creatures groaning and shuffling among the tombstones with their shovels, torches, and appropriate floral tributes. —*Shirley Gumert*
Santa Fe, N.M.

Aunt Izzy smiled with fanatical conviction, spittle flecking her withered, dry lips, her gnarled hand gripping the smooth wooden handle of the handy-dandy hatchet with its genuine stainless-steel blade (recently purchased for only $9.99) and with a small, insane cry raised it above her graying head and brought it down, down, down, upon the salesman's foot, wedged securely in the front door.

—*B. J. Davenport*
Las Vegas, Nev.

Harry kills mice with a hammer as part of his poetry readings, but we're still pals.

—*Kyle J. Spiller*
Garden Grove, Calif.

Humming a cheerful tune, Millicent continued removing the organs from the body, rinsing them, patting them dry with a thick terry towel, then placing them gently in Jeff's Li'l Playmate cooler, all the while wondering what he'd think of her single brilliant solution to two nagging problems—his mother and her constant and bitter complaints about Millicent's neglecting her, and Jeff's repeatedly verbalized wish for something in his lunch besides peanut butter and jelly sandwiches.

—*Deanna D. Ledgett*
Riverside, Calif.

Emily had always liked little John, the neighbors' kid, and he was particularly good done this way in a delicate béchamel sauce with simmered mushrooms and just a hint of garlic.

—*Jill Rose*
Captain Cook, Hawaii

LYTTONY II

"FROM A SIMPLE PEASANT TO
THE HEIMLICH MANEUVER
AND THE
FAITHLESS SNORKELER."

André, a simple peasant, had only one thing on his mind as he crept along the east wall: "André creep . . . André creep . . . André creep."

—David Allen Janzen
Davis, Calif.

Alone with the doctor, a small computer located in a booth at the rear of the drugstore, Angel read the diagnosis from the short printed sheet: "Terminally ill—you have less than a year—please detach bill from bottom half and pay as soon as possible."

—Roxy Kelley
Anacortes, Wash.

Gogerty gazed out of the laboratory window on the third floor of the Museum of Natural History and wondered how many more goddam otters he would have to stretch.

—Craig Marshall Smith
Aurora, Colo.

Mary looked up from playing with the basket of kittens to hear her instructor repeat, "Remember, kitten in the left hand, skinning knife in the right!"

—R. W. O'Bryan
Perrysberg, Ohio

Dr. Chet Wheatfield fumbled with his gold lighter, coughed, saw his half-lit cigarette fall from his lips into his cold quiche, and swore softly as the double Cutty Sark he had knocked over with his elbow ran down the crease of his pant leg and oozed into his Gucci loafer, reminding that he had really done it—only hours earlier he had actually performed the world's first successful brain transplant.

—James Macdonald
Vancouver, B.C.

It was a real jolt, you know, to hear whassis-name say those holy words so . . . so . . . so dirty-like, you know, while they tossed my best buddy's remains, urn and all, out of the sunroof at 55 mph.
—*Leighton L. Smith*
Vienna, Va.

As the nurse injected the vital medication needed to cure Lars of his highly contagious, and fatal, disease, he could feel the lamb chops and potato salad he had eaten the night before slowly disintegrating into the proteins and carbohydrates needed for the next day's journey to Tacoma.
—*Emily Slatten*
Lafayette, Calif.

I was an extremely extremely extremely sensitive child.
—*Arnold Rosenfeld*
Austin, Tex.

As the velvet squid wrapped its cold, mossy tentacles ever more tightly around her lower limbs, Alicia ceased her struggles, and loosening her grasp on her high school ring, she let it fall into the depths of the aquamarine waters surrounding Catalina Island, murmuring weakly, "Let it lie there, as my broken body will lie, alone and abandoned, a puzzle to the glass-bottom boats and an eternal reproach to my fiancé, that faithless snorkeler."
—*Anne Pautler*
Santa Monica, Calif.

Our story is best begun at its end—for then was it done—there could be no turning back—and for a fleeting moment time stopped breathing for Bill as the enormity of passion that had swelled and ebbed through his life loomed before him anew: the women (Ethel, Sophie, Jo); the wine (he drank only white table);

the songs ("Tie a yellow ribbon . . ."); the good times with Fred and Harry . . . all in vivid colors . . . all wrapped in those tropical scents which, his closest friends knew, had long characterized his particular lust for life (impregnating his collection of short-sleeved pastel rayon dress shirts) as now he hurtled off Al's Hay and Grain, cartwheeling in desperation to the egg-frying pavement that was County-Clerksville in August one story below, finally leaving a mark that would endure until the large coarse brown rotating brooms of the DPW truck wiped clean the stain that was his legacy.　　　　　—*Michael Mintz*
Lafayette, Calif.

Alone in his small flat, a piece of roast beef sandwich lodged deeply in his fleshy throat, Martin performed the Heimlich maneuver upon himself, spat the sodden lump of beef and bread upon the wall near the stove, burped—and soon felt much better.　　　　　—*Brian Boldt*
Cotati, Calif.

A whippoorwill somewhere miles away in the secluded valley below called its sad, sorrowful call, underscoring the loneliness and isolation of the remote mountain ledge, and Samantha Jane dropped her piton and gazed in open-mouthed horror at the brazen chipmunk already snatching the trail mix that spilled down Bucky's red Eddie Bauer shirt, silently chastising herself, as the sobs welled up, for not paying attention when they demonstrated the Heimlich maneuver.　　　　　—*Denis W. Wade*
San Francisco, Calif.

THE WAY
WE LIVE
NOW

"NO OTHER WRITER
HAS FULLY CAPTURED
THE ELUSIVE ESSENCE
OF AMERICAN LIFE
IN THE '80S
—ITS DIVERSITY,
ITS COMPLEXITY,
ITS PROMISE,
ITS DANGER,
ITS FRAGILITY
—BUT WHO'S READY
FOR IT ANYWAY, SO
TRY THIS BOOK."

"I want something more in life," Welsley fumed as the lime-scented Jacuzzi bubbles collected between his secretary's breasts.
—*Josh T. Simpson*
Bloomfield Hills, Mich.

Feeling not a little trepidant, his hands grappling with the flat-ware array before him, Hasel finally culled from the collection a soup spoon—not the right choice for sampling caviar, as he soon saw from the livid look Monya shot him.   —*Jeffrey Sketchley*
Dublin, Calif.

Desirée had it all: family, money, power, lovers, a golden re-triever, and herpes.   —*David L. Baker*
Georgetown, Ky.

It was only as Pamela entered the eighth department store, with its warm holiday glow, the throngs of Christmas shoppers, and the Andrews Sisters still singing "Frosty the Snowman," that she realized that if they did have a Cabbage Patch doll she was going to strangle the little bastard, throw its lumpy body in some slush-filled gutter, and send in a false name on the adoption cer-tificate.   —*John E. Rogers*
Washington, D.C.

Those of us who were witnesses the night the cat learned to open the gerbil cage have that event etched in our memories for-ever.   —*Mary A. Anthony*
Grand Rapids, Mich.

"Skeeter" Turpin kneeled in the bathroom of the La Jolla Budget Inn Executive Suite, frantically searching for the dollar-off coupon that he had cheerfully been given when he registered

at the front desk, and that had now floatingly slipped behind the alabaster commode, entitling him to a cash discount on any drink in the lounge, located under the stairway next to the ice machine, during happy hour, when suddenly—the phone, sitting on the nightstand next to the Gideon Bible, rang loudly, causing him to smack the back of his head on the sink.   —*Mac Sigler*
Hattiesburg, Miss.

She was a definite "10": a "5" with a high-paying job.
—*Cole B. Kiser*
Centerville, Ohio

Jeremy Felspar, flinty veteran of the 1973 Arab oil embargo, awoke with a screech from a somnolent sleep, the machine-gunesque clatter of the modest tan and gray Big Ben bedside alarm at the side of his bed kicking him in the groin of his inner ear, and was, after a few moments, instantaneously overwhelmed with a vague feeling of dreadful angst, that dreadful feeling of vagueness which, even now, forced a question into his anxious mind, just as a badger forces his mucus-coated snout into the den of some lesser beast—should he call in sick?
—*Rob E. Nelson*
Colorado Springs, Colo.

Meeting unexpectedly at the salad bar, the ménage à trois of the late twentieth century—adoptive mother, birth mother, and beloved child—exchanged suspicious looks across the sneeze shield.   —*Judith E. Harris*
Sitka, Alaska

Once upon a Tuesday in some long past November with the sun dripping orangely on the Kremlin-shaped cumuli, my baby-

smooth footsies kerplopped convincingly upon the purple bathroom throw rug (it was, more accurately, mauve) as I listened almost unconsciously yet with great strain for the unmistakable "ching-chong-ching-chong" that meant (and could only mean) the onset of a new day at the beleaguered and oft-maligned Sioux City Taco Bell.   —*Ciscoe Louis*
                                        Jamaica Plain, Mass.

"Jason . . . Jason . . . Jason . . . Jason . . . Jason . . . Jason . . ." intoned Coach Brown as he called the roll for his third-grade gym class.   —*Ronald R. Kyser*
                                        Oneonta, N.Y.

After six months of firing off anecdotes to *Reader's Digest* and not receiving even one acceptance, Gusha had used up all her own stories and those of her relatives and friends and had taken to hiding in restaurant booths to eavesdrop on strangers when the inevitable happened.   —*Mary Brown*
                                        Ventura, Calif.

Whilst sitting on my balcony in the late afternoon, sipping my gin and tonic and watching my youngest daughter, Katrina, idly flicking stones at the houseboy whilst he watered the potted plants, it struck me that perhaps I had wasted my life.
                                        —*Kenneth J. Hall*
                                        Sumatra, Indonesia

THE WAY
WE LOVE
NOW

"SHE WAS
TRAPPED BY LONGING,
ENSLAVED BY PASSION,
BRANDED BY DESIRE,
THEN LOVE
NOTCHED HER EARS."

It was a sultry midnight in the tropics and the moon hung list-lessly in a myriad of stars as Marian caressed Roger's neck—a neck moist with the perspiration of his impassioned embrace—and wondered, her thoughts careening rapidly from one possibil-ity to another, Roger who?   —*Mary M. Gleitner*
Chicago, Ill.

Angie wondered how she'd explain to Bertram that she couldn't "put her coat on and head home"—as she knew he'd in-sist she do, once he'd concluded his after-a-date attempt at pas-sion, with his usual boring, endless kiss—because the gum she'd stuck on the underside of her left wrist, to be able to kiss him at all, was now firmly enmeshed in the uneven, prickly black hair at the base of his neck, and the broken link of her ten-year-old gold watch was also hooked on a loose thread of the frayed collar of his blue checkered shirt.   —*Ludela Hansen*
Wilmington, Del.

The waitress's eyes shone like the fabric of his cheap, thread-bare trousers, and even as she sloshed hot coffee on them, mut-tering an absent-minded "Oops!" in apology, Duffy knew that someday she would be pouring java in his home.
—*Ann Rhodes Conley*
Pittsburgh, Pa.

She sighed lustily, as he pulled up his camouflage Y-fronts by their frayed elastic, then scratched the pimples scattered among the sparse, limp hairs on his mottled pigeon chest, while the steaming samovar misted the windows.   —*Peter John Athey*
Versailles, France

As Howard watched the virgin sun streak a brilliant stripe across the velvet water, he was reminded of the neat precision of the zipper on Sylvia's designer jeans.   —*Lois Briggs*
Seal Beach, Calif.

Amanda couldn't decide—should she give up her study of menstrual imagery in Hopi folklore (which no one else on that sedate Midwestern campus had thought to look into) and settle down to a nice quiet life with Philip on the farm, where together with the plowing and the planting the two of them could experience nature's timeless rhythms firsthand, or should she go to law school?   —*Robert Massa*
New York, N.Y.

"Trust you?" she exclaimed, her shoulders heaving in heavy sobs as she hunched her back to him over the stove, the stirring motions in the pan of pasta sauce raggedly harmonizing with the stirrings in her heart, the bright red sauce vividly reminding her of the slashes of bright red lipstick on his collar, her tears flowing, adding bitter sweetness to the pungent garlic taste of the reminding sauce, "trust you?"   —*William W. Finlaw, Jr.*
Tallahassee, Fla.

Tom stopped picking the fuzz of Linda's angora sweater off his shirt, glanced up to see Linda clomp out of their hideously well-decorated bedroom carrying her ferns and his Don Ho albums, and felt a cold chill go up his spine as he realized that he did not know how to operate the microwave oven.
—*Lucian Janik, Jr.*
Somerdale, N.J.

"Why, you silly little pussycat," he chuckled warmly, "of course I'll make love to you!"   —*W. R. C. Shedenhelm*
Ventura, Calif.

Damien Dutspmil smiled in simmering suspense as he stood, his wife-to-be lying limply across his left arm, under the inflatable baroque pearl-colored canopy of Deacon Dougie Don Dominican's Discount House of Retail Rubber Ware & Wedding Chapel—whose motto, "Repose on your matrimonial river with our life raft of love," was regally festooned above an unemotional storefront near downtown Reno—and wondered just how soon the fair deacon, who had lost his sight in a socially unacceptable yet self-fulfilling experience (it was in all the papers!), would present him with his complimentary cannister of compressed CO_2 while saying that lovely and long-awaited phrase: "You may now inflate the bride."   —*Stephen H. Brown*
Half Moon Bay, Calif.

It was several languid moments before Labina realized that the light streaming across her sleep-swollen eyes and bruised lips was not from the golden sunshine that made California so famous along with oranges and sweatpants, but was from the bathroom, where he had left the water dripping and the toilet seat up without even saying good-bye.   —*Kristiana Gregory*
Pocatello, Idaho

It was more than right, Ronald thought pensively as he gazed down at the canine corpse bleeding at his feet, that Margaret should shoot Muffy—the little dog had been instrumental in bringing them together on that distant day when, as a frolicking puppy, he had tangled his leash around her pretty ankles—but

doing it on the Persian rug displayed a vindictiveness he could not easily forgive. —*David Kasserman*
Haddonfield, N.J.

It was not the first time I had driven a man mad (though some had admittedly gotten no further than a state of mild irritability, and some remained merely peckish) by removing my cap to unleash a torrent of sable hair across my ivory shoulders (lest there be any confusion, my own hair, emerging in the usual way, from my scalp). —*Tori Twersky*
Campbell, Calif.

Clad in a light summer frock, the mauve print which James gave her when James was still interested in frocks and she in James, Vera sits brooding at the tea table and stirs a cup of what she expects is execrable Irish Breakfast, wondering why it is that when one's lovers become one's friends the resulting social discomfiture is impalpably but inescapably less intriguing than the sequestered malaise which results from the reverse.

—*Deborah Wessell*
Seattle, Wash.

After fourteen days of intense, nonstop, leave-the-food-at-the-door lovemaking in the honeymoon suite of the Pocono Hilton Hotel, she wasn't sure she liked her groom with a beard, but after fourteen days of intense, nonstop, leave-the-food-at-the-door lovemaking in the honeymoon suite of the Pocono Hilton Hotel she also wasn't sure she liked her groom at all, and she quickly decided the first thing she would do when she left this overrated bordello was to hire someone else to take care of her horses.

—*Helene Story*
Sacramento, Calif.

I pray that Majorie can find the courage to accept what must happen, Lloyd thought, his heart pounding like a washing machine full of galoshes at the prospect of leaving his beloved secretary and confidante, the only woman he had ever known who was both trustworthy and grammatically conservative.

—*Steve Aydelott*
Denver, Colo.

At thirty-five, Lucius Burbank seemed content as head of the Germination Testing Department of a large seed company, being short, slight of build, and—yes—unattractive, and he showed no interest in the opposite sex *until* the morning of April 27, 1981, when his young secretary—the blond, the long-legged and luscious Miss Langley—emerged from the bathroom with the back of her white mini-skirt inadvertently tucked inside the elastic top of her Underalls.
—*Robert Nottke*
Dundee, Ill.

Watching the wanton whale frolicking in the azure-blue sea off the coast of Mendocino, Dorrick ruminated on the incredible year past, not without some amusement, and then, hesitating only a moment before turning to his wife, Griselda, waiting fretful as a fiddler beside him, he murmured, "Don't they remind you of us, dear?"
—*Terry O'Neal*
Morgan Hill, Calif.

THE DEADER THEY DIE

"REX MALLARD KNEW
THE COPS WERE WRONG
WHEN THEY RULED
HIS PARTNER'S DEATH
A SUICIDE
—AFTER ALL, HE'D
KILLED HIM HIMSELF."

My bank account was emptier than a housefly's bladder on that Monday morning when across the threshold of "Nick Blunt, Inquiries" oozed a dame like something in one of those magazines you only read when you've gone through all the old *Newsweeks* in your dentist's office, I mean to tell you a dame stacked like a load of library books in the arms of some four-eyed kid, with her assets packed inside some simple, little red-sequined number that clung to her the way a Hollywood actor hangs on to his Valium prescription and that probably cost hardly any more than moo goo gai pan cooked by the Dalai Lama, a dame with trouble written all over her as if it were the name of some ritzy fashion designer, and a dame who gave me, when I swung my ten-year-old wing tips off my desk and admitted yeah, I was Blunt, the kind of look you might give a nun buying a diaphragm.

(from *The Deader They Die*)   —*L. H. Sintetos*
                                          Santa Cruz, Calif.

I been a private Ricardo for forty years, so I seen some goddam ugly messes in my sweet life, but nothing like what happened to Dakota Joe—he looked like he'd swallowed a live bobcat, then done something to piss it off.   —*Robin Wood*
                                          Pinole, Calif.

The Luger pressed steely-hard against my side and sweat dripped off my forehead as I crouched between the marabou robe and leopard coat, peering through the keyhole at the blonde in the boudoir, and realized, with a spasm in my gut, that I was in the wrong apartment—the butterfly tattoo on Big Eddie's broad was on her right cheek.   —*Laura Ferguson*
                                          Salem, Oreg.

It was raining like an orphaned rat's tears the night the blonde bounced into my office and my eyes popped out at her pulchritude like hard-boiled grapes; "That's what women are made for," I said to myself as I collated her curves through the cigarette smoke and fingered my .45. —*Fred Manget*
Stone Mountain, Ga.

The gray Chevy Nova sedan appeared from a side street in a scrunching swerve, but I was back far enough that I still couldn't see the license number, so I sped closer—snatching at the slip of paper on the seat that would have the tag number that should be on the gray sedan—only to see that the tag number on the paper didn't match up with that of the gray sedan that I was fast bearing down on because the accelerator pedal on my old green Olds coupe was stuck down to the floor. —*George Carley Safford*
Topeka, Kans.

The first thing I thought when she swayed into my office, dressed in about enough silk and lace to upholster a throw pillow, maybe, was that I hadn't seen a body built like that since they quit making Studebakers, and the second thing was that this dame couldn't possibly have enough skirt to hide the .38 she was now pointing in the general direction of my Fruit-of-the-Looms.
—*Ray C. Gainey*
Indianapolis, Ind.

The blonde strode the length of the pier with those solid-gold legs, high heels clicking, trailing every male eye for a block around, until she reached the end where my houseboat *The Inside Straight* rode in barnacled mournfulness, its bulwarks creaking as it rocked to the swells pushed up by the passing of the yachts of the cocaine kings, contemptuous as medieval lords of the jaundiced scrutiny of one broken-down private dick.

—*Tom Eaton*
Kansas City, Mo.

The first time I saw her, at the bar-of-no-name, it was across a sea of faces—bodies treading water, mouths swallowing air above the wine, the vodka, and the brandied promises of salvation—as, finding my eyes, she held them with hers, like a hypnotist, her crimson lips, across the abyss, forming words I could suddenly read as the deaf do: HELP ME PLEASE; those were the first words she spoke, with no sound, the first time I saw her, at the bar-of-no-name.

—*Bonnie Hearn*
Fresno, Calif.

You'd've had to be blind or lactophobic not to know that the stuff framing Fat Frankie Juke's sausage-like lips was chocolate milk and Vic Revolver was neither, but he knew Fat Frank was a vino man, the redder the better, and though he'd spent his share of bourbon nights Vic couldn't recall ever seeing the Juke sleeping this way, under the marquee of the Kat Fong Arcade at three A.M. with the neon words "Dim Sum" reflecting in his cloudy eyes and chopsticks protruding from his ears.

—*Jim H. Smith*
Seattle, Wash.

She appeared before me like an adolescent fantasy, fixing me with a sidelong stare as cold as a Midwest morning in February, her hands balled up into tiny fists on her naked hips, pushing back the silver fox coat which was sliding off her alabaster shoulders while her right foot pivoted peevishly on a six-inch heel, and as I flipped off the intercom after telling my secretary to knock

off early, I did what any other shamus who was having his libido flame-broiled would do—I fell in love. —*Ed Tootill*
Philadelphia, Pa.

My partner had warned me that she was the kind of dame who could bite the cojones off a musk ox without stopping to stub out her cigarette, but when Lady Kahooinor Rexalli dissolved into snuffingly piteous sobs in my surprised embrace I couldn't help feeling—briefly, to be sure, for passion is a fantasy not easily trusted by an old, hardened gumshoe like yours truly, Peter Patter—that she was nothing more than a damned scared skinny kid underneath her million-dollar makeup and her ten-pound diamond rings. —*Sharron Cohen*
Gloucester, Mass.

Long before the slinky babe in the polka-dot sweater oozed into his office, he knew she'd show up—and show up just when he was down to his last pair of clean shorts. —*Jan Butchart*
Waukesha, Wis.

I knew it wasn't going to be one of my more enjoyable days when, as I was getting behind the wheel of my Impala, Benny Wisniewski—aka Eunice Menkowitz—slid in beside me and, jabbing the cavernous barrel of an overworked .45 in my ribs, asked, "How's the vasectomy, toots?" —*Eugene Jones, Jr.*
Milwaukee, Wis.

Awakening abruptly to the foreign taste of the dog's foot in his mouth, an untimely interruption to an erotic dream which was an extension of the previous evening's late-night movie, McBrawley's forearm propelled the animal in an unplanned trajectory toward the Playboy calendar tacked above the door, barely missing the petite blond intruder who had originally startled the animal, but fatefully causing poochie to intercept the bullet from her gun which would have otherwise ended this and all future dreams.

—*Oliver Watson III*
Orange, Calif.

The fresh memory of her stupendous breasts jackhammered his woman-jangled nerves, and as Johnny Gumshoe buried his face in his seventh cup of stale coffee the truth blasted him with sawed-off horror, splattering clue-wracked, booze-dulled thoughts all over the pavement of his brain: it was Monday morning after his vacation in Guerrero with Sadie the Stripper, and the coffee he'd been drinking was at least a week old.

—*Dale Newton*
Portland, Ore.

The well-muscled, deeply tanned, plaid-suited, patent leather-shod shamus Chance Chisel strode purposefully into the Happy Hour Bar and spotted her, a busty, catlike, black-haired, olive-skinned, leggy beauty of a girl sitting under the flashing neon—a most provocative artifact made up of two red H's, one atop the other, the left side of the upper H continuing downward to be the right side of the lower H, thus forming what? . . . a symbol? an esoteric allusion? an emblematic assertion of the interdependence of opposites—heaven and hell? hep and hokey? hemorrhoids and halitosis?—and said to her, "Chance, not perfection, rules the world—wanna sin a bit?"

—*Stephen Schwandt*
Minneapolis, Minn.

PLAIN BROWN WRAPPERS

"A PROBING, INTRUDING,
MEDDLING NOVEL
WHICH DARES TO ASK
THE QUESTION:
HOW MUCH ARE YOU
WILLING TO PAY
FOR CHEAP FICTION?"

Although Bunny Muffet knew her life was bound to change after her private parts were declared public recreation areas by the Glendale Chamber of Commerce, she was unprepared for the 101 red-faced, pot-bellied tourists who arrived in chartered buses the following morning, eager to negotiate the ample curves and explore the lush regions of Glendale's best-loved natural resource.
—*Lynn Chiodini*
Seattle, Wash.

Jack's hot, hairy hands mauled his sister-in-law Georgette's thin, gossamer blouse as she bent her willing thighs to his burning need; she closed her eyes and steamily breathed, "Oh, kiss me, Jack, and make it hurt!"—but had she opened her eyes and seen the uncertainty on his face, she might have guessed he was thinking, "Kiss you? We shouldn't even be doing this."
—*Stephen Seitz*
Arlington, Va.

Young Elwell Overton's mama had told him many times that wakefulness is best cured by *counting* sheep; but he just knew he would have to be a damn fool to keep track of hundreds, or even thousands, of the woolly critters every night when, his way, six or seven, tops, put him out until morning. —*Ashley Sellick*
Wallace, Nova Scotia

"You can call it 'a celebration of life' all you want," said Snow White caustically to the seven little men looking up at her, "to me it sounds suspiciously like a gang-bang!"—*Robert F. Pollock*
Newton, Mass.

The feckless, thin-shanked lad sat speechless on the park bench, palms sweating, throat dry, watching the buxom maidens

sashay past, their opulent breasts undulating under the thin gauze of their blouses, when a toothless old crone gave him a sharp dig in the ribs with her bony elbow and hissed, "Whistle, you dumb bastard!"
— *Barbara C. Kroll*
Kennett Square, Pa.

Captain Bedloe Beauregard III finished drinking his mint julep in the sun-drenched, porticoed porch of the mansion overlooking the immense cotton fields, deposited his still frosted glass upon the wicker table, and, without breaking his stride, carried Miss Lulubelle bodily into her dainty, frilled bedroom, where, with all the ardor and intensity that would later help him carve a niche for his name in the annals of American history in less dainty environments such as Shenandoah, Shiloh, and Appomattox, he proceeded to pluck Miss Lulubelle of her virginity, plundering and ravaging her immaculate bosom wherein her pure heart fluttered wildly like a scared finch imprisoned in a stout ribbed cage, while in her mind a single thought drummed endlessly: "On a scale of one to ten, I'd give him three, tops. . . ."
— *Jose A. Lourenco*
Lisbon, Portugal

The cat was washing his butt in front of company again, and Joe and Sue shifted uneasily on the couch, both of them caught up in the tiresome, tedious task of offering some sort of disguised distraction to their guests.
— *Rosemary McGuffin*
Huntington, W.Va.

Shiveringly, Bliss lay under the bed with hopeless abandon, while above, churlish Derek tempestuously made violent, headstrong love to Mira, her personal lady's maid for several years, who suffered from an unrelenting, brutal case of acne of the but-

tocks which had kept her from performing her maidly duties for
many weeks on end.
                                                        —*Jean Lewis*
                                                    Saratoga, Calif.

Marietta had known many men—Charles, whose Southern
chivalry could not excuse his theft of her most priceless possession; Liam, whose attempts to sell her into white slavery belied
his smiling green eyes and boyish charm; Ashton, whose weak
chin and irresolute manner confirmed his public-school-bred ad-
diction to the abominable crime against nature; Philippe, whose
penchant for ménages à trois made Marietta feel like a third
wheel; Juan, whose jealousy and suspicion kept her a prisoner on
his lush, tropical plantation; Ali, the handsome Moroccan whose
many wives gave her intimate attention; Mario, the simple Sici-
lian shepherd who loved Marietta second only to his sheep;
Nikos, whose sexual habits harked back to his Greek heritage;
Yuri, who was as hard and cold as the Russian winter; Wilhelm,
whose brutal and sadistic proclivities were revealed by his ex-
cessive fondness for jack boots and riding crops, among others—
but no one was like Alexander der Carmichael; in order to win his
love, Marietta vowed to overlook his herpes and come to his bed
a virgin.
                                                    —*M. Allain Bauduit*
                                                    Mount Vernon, N.Y.

Glamorous, gutsy Genevieve slid effortlessly down the pole as
slobbering dogs with masks of men circled stealthily, looking up
her dress, making low gurgling noises from the bottom of their
throats, licking their inner lips and the sides of their teeth.
                                                    —*Jeffrey Scott Brown*
                                                    Joe Jost's, Calif.

"Jiminy Cricket, that feels good!" he ejaculated, fitting a fresh codpiece, which had been carefully selected from his well-hung wardrobe.

—*Michael Karp*
Dorval, Quebec

When the sap runs high in the Sago-Sago, the white owls fly in circles, and the men come indoors tugging at their belts and asking for meat, you know that the rutting season has begun.

—*Olive C. R. Smith*
Irvine, Calif.

Still flushed and quivering like a rabbit at bay with the memory of that afternoon's turbulent and illicit passions, Natalie Tingelstad set down her grocery sack—containing the packages of now thawed-into-mulch spinach, the reproaching salami for her small vulnerable son Jimmy's lunchbox sandwiches, the frosting-in-a-can for her unemployed husband Mitchell's fortieth birthday cake, and the sundry small necessities that made up the fabric of their common life—and guiltily hoped that her inoffensive albeit bromidic husband, now unsuspectingly ironing her jogging shorts as he watched the Rams game, would not discover—as she had just realized—that the new lace-trimmed, pink acetate underpants she had put on that morning not only were now on backward but had also been ripped to shreds.

(from *The Long Hot Liberated Summer of Natalie Tingelstad*)

—*L. H. Sintetos*
Santa Cruz, Calif.

Captain Hezekiah Hornpipe, lately master of the whaling bark *Priapus*, had not slept soundly since that bleak September morn on the Arctic Ocean when the great white sperm had crushed his dinghy, scattering seamen across the waves.

> —*Lawrence Dorr*
> *San Francisco, Calif.*

Her near-perfect features failed to reflect accurately the sickening sensation comprised of equal portions of frustration and sheer horror that wafted over her like clinging, fetid waves of opaque, stagnant water; lying supine—arms and legs akimbo—on the rumpled, plum-hued satin sheets that suffused the bleak, cold starlight, she grasped the sesquipedalian metal-and-plastic intruder in both of her meticulously manicured hands, bemoaning her wretched fate to Sappho, Diana, and anyone else who would listen—Evelyn had totally forgotten the batteries.

> —*Cedric R. Braun*
> *San Jose, Calif.*

As the hulking animal approached her, with his appendage preceding by what seemed more than mere inches, voluptuous Veronica Vandervule, seduced by erotic sights, sounds, and smells, found herself thinking that, if people did come to look like their pets, then Rangee, the elephant trainer, deserved her undivided attention.

> —*Georgie C. Bell*
> *Burlington, Wash.*

He pounded his seed-filled zucchini into her well-oiled food processor and she took him through all the cycles, puréeing his once proud squash.

> —*Joe Galliani*
> *Long Beach, Calif.*

Parked at the scenic overlook, Buffy, already quite guilt-ridden, gapingly stared at Max in disbelief as he stood, shouting gleefully out the moon roof of his father's BMW 318i to all within the shadow of Make-out Mountain: "Trousers 'round my ankles, buns shimmering in starlight, she couldn't understand why I was howling into the night." —*Frank R. Adams III*
Pensacola, Fla.

She thrashed and bolted under him like a high-spirited horse as the winds picked up fury and a thunderhead moved in over the stables, and the two lovers' hoarse breathing matched the racing wind as Tony's jockey shorts stretched to their limit around his ankles and the lightning's whip-like crackle spurred them on to an exciting finish. —*Larry D. Kohlhorst*
Sylvania, Ohio

The teepee was dark and stuffy, and the blanket on which they lay was scratchy and reeked faintly of horse dung, but Belinda, swooning with ecstasy amidst her cast-off crinolines, noticed none of this, in her triumphant awareness that Charging Bull had made a woman of her at last. —*Paula Lozar*
San Jose, Calif.

"I really feel that 'a few hours of home study' is insufficient training to qualify you to perform my gynecological examination," Brenda Feldman whispered breathlessly to the lump under the sheet which indicated the present position of the brilliant dwarf, Esteban. —*Robert F. Pollock*
Newton, Mass.

Transfixed by the relentless thrust of the massive steel blade against the embankment, the two huddled for a moment in the cab of the snorting, yellow bulldozer before he roused himself to murmur, "Guapa—little rabbit—did you feel the earth move?"

—*H. Winton Ellingsworth*
Tulsa, Okla.

LYTTONY III

"FROM CELLULITE TO
PETRI DISHES AND
FROM HAROLD BUTTS
TO EARL GREY"

Love really is a many-splendored thing, Mamba thought to herself as Thad shoved another handful of peanuts up her trunk.

—*Eric Sandstrom*
Peoria, Ill.

Much to the consternation of his next-of-kin, Houghton R. Rainsworth IV had been intestate the day he impatiently pressed the accelerator pedal of his sleek, polished Jaguar to the floor, reaching 140 miles per hour before his vehicle struck a hedgehog and went airborne, making two elegant gyres and then landing on its roof and smashing Rainsworth as flat as the mashed-in faces of the Chinese pugs he had been fond of raising at Eton.

—*David Willingham*
Georgetown, Tenn.

Stuffing his left hind hoof into the stirrup at belly height, the innovative Champion played footsie with his Lordship's left boot, the while he raced along on three legs, in good time, too, considering that the Master suddenly decided to also hold hands with his polished hoof, meanwhile lolling heavily to port, like any common lackey, unbalancing the whole delicate maneuver at the speed of light . . .

—*Alfhild Wallen*
Duncan Mills, Calif.

Dancer-grammarians that they were, Julia and Karinov were singularly magnetized by the plurality of each other's leaps, and became vocative, dative, genitive; and, lo, as the music swelled, K. rose, imperative, to his full six-feet-nine, wound his neck about hers like a trumpeter swan, and idiomaticized, "Punctuate me, baby!" as he, overcome, lapsed into a passive subjunctive pas.

—*Lucy Lightbody*
Troy, Mich.

Shimmying her multi-layers of cellulite in a burst of liberating clairvoyance, Bernice squished the suitcase she had packed for her weekend at the Zen center.

—*Sibyl Darter*
Granada Hills, Calif.

The cellulite on Bertha's thighs rippled in the wind as she stood on the beach watching the icy waves on Lake Michigan lunging toward the shore. —*Kay Mitchell*
Hindsdale, Ill.

He came home from school on the afternoon of April 25, 1972, and turned on his radio to hear Foster Hewitt's broadcast of the fourth game of the Stanley Cup semifinals between Boston and St. Louis, when the thought suddenly hit him—what was Foster Hewitt doing broadcasting a game between Boston and St. Louis?
—*Jack Morrow*
Edmonton, Alberta

It was an obscure, an obfuscating night, a night for obstreperous obloquies, thought Occam, as he applied his razor to the pulchritudinous pomme, which Adam had alotted to the lot; and he directed those obnoxious obloquies to the source of his eruptive spleen, Mr. Motley Cruz . . . applying his razor with venomous vengeance all the while.
—*Dr. Marlene Caroselli*
Pacific Palisades, Calif.

The darkly handsome Bosworth Cranston sauntered expectantly into his wedding rehearsal dinner with arrogance and confidence befitting a man considered the most eligible bachelor by the "Who's Who" of the Newport Beach Social Register, and who would have been perfect had it not been for the small, but insistent, green leafy vegetable fragment that was always wedged between his two flawless front teeth; there, Eunice, his exquisitely beautiful and almost perfect fiancée, whose only flaw was oddly enough remarkably similar to that of Bosworth, eagerly waited with breathless anticipation to embark upon a lifetime relationship, which unknown to either of them was of an incestuous nature due to a gynecological experiment on identical twins that went awry, because Bosworth's and Eunice's story really began in a petri dish in a seedy and poorly ventilated back room of a decertified obstetrician in Mule Shoe, Texas.

—*Carol Haas-Turman*
Albuquerque, N.M.

Twins have always run in our family, but when Great-aunt Gus dropped triplets after four straight sets of twins, the MacGurdy family tradition known as "culling" was born.

—*Cecily Korell*
Arcadia, Calif.

"You titillate me, Humphrey, old hoss," lisped Lady Licentia languidly, as she softly stirred her Earl Grey with a limpid hand, "and I'll titillate you."

—*Tom Willis*
Seminole, Fla.

Harold Butts, coach of the Missisoggi Doggi aerobics team and captain of the Missisoggi Home for the Aged interdisciplinary team for promoting independent bowel function, pulled his Misty Harbor trench coat collar up past his ears and his Misty Harbor trench coat collar down over his eyes as he added the package of X-lax to his supermarket cart, certain that his future in Missisoggi, a hamlet so isolated from the mainstream that the

nearest McDonald's was sixty miles to the east and the nearest Sears store almost eighty miles to the north, would become utterly unbearable should any of his pupils, patients, or teammates discover his action.   —*Judith Hays*
                                                          Wichita, Kans.

Were I not in my ninety-seventh year, looking out through rheumy eyes at nubile young bodies clothed in "fast-zip jeans" and "one-pull tank tops" and thinking back to my youthful, Victorian struggles with whale-boned corsets, "hook-and-eyed" bodices, ribboned knots that would not come undone, laced bustles that would not come unlaced, and yards and yards and yards of crinoline that formed a "maze" that groping hand could not unravel, I would be filled with jealousy and bitterness at the ease of conquest today, were I not in my ninety-seventh year, looking out through rheumy eyes at nubile young bodies clothed in "fast-zip jeans" and "one-pull tank tops" . . . Oh, to hell with it!!
                                                    —*Edward H. Haynes*
                                                          Dillon, Colo.

In the heat of the moment, he always did what he had to do; yet later, surrounded by the wood panels and brandy snifters of the secret room that housed his very private collection, Raoul wryly reflected that he might well have been more discreet than to remove the ruby-encrusted, myth-enshrouded tiara from the granite head of Councilman Smithers in the town square of sleepy Corn Row, Iowa.   —*Kathy Peltzman*
                                                          Prior Lake, Minn.

Black grease dissolved from under Eddie's fingernail into his now-cold coffee as he resigned himself to the emergency of the drowning green bottle-fly—a necessity which distracted him

from counting the hammered-head tacks missing from the yellowed Naugahyde on the next stool . . . and, like finding metal chips in your transmission pan, drove home the inescapable realization that his luck hadn't changed. —*Mario Vasquez*
Long Beach, Calif.

It was only when Hagedorn, listing a bit himself atop the fogbound windy bluff, reached under his fleece-lined kilt and pulled out the cinch bag that he choked down the bolus of saliva and became cognizant of her all-too-devious plan to wrest the crown from Uncle Nemo and fly away with the dapper but diminutive Mr. Doodles. —*Will Conway*
Dover, N.H.

ROMANCE: HISTORICAL, GOTHIC, AND GENERIC

"HIS POWER
MATCHED HER PRIDE;
HER BEAUTY MATCHED
HIS BOLDNESS,
HIS CUFF-LINKS
MATCHED
HER EARRINGS."

Astride the rhythmically pulsating flanks of her galloping mount, Lady Ashcroft plunged into the dark, moistly warm forest, breathlessly bolted past the ancient plundered fortress once torn asunder by Saxon stones, came upon the jagged cliffs that pierced the brooding skies, where far below the surging waves relentlessly assaulted the mist-shrouded cove, and there she gravely pondered why Lord Ashcroft was always thinking about sex.
—*Craig Nagoshi*
Boulder, Colo.

Lady Fernalee Smythdon-Billowingsbreth perceived her tiny dragon-skin slipper catching and rending the ecru, cobweb-lace, heirloom petticoat bequeathed her by her husband's late great-aunt Venetia Vivefors-Vinesquier as she hurriedly readied herself for the All-Elves' Eve Ball even now being preluded by His Highness's finest Royal Pipers, violists, flutists, and precision percussionists.
—*Sandra Thomas*
Colorado Springs, Colo.

As his mouth hungrily sought hers, she gasped as if drowning, her bosom surging above the jewel-encrusted stomacher, twin nacreous blancmanges cast up by the storm within her.
—*Barry R. Paull*
Santa Ana, Calif.

She panted heavily as Lord Nigel drew her to him, not daring to believe that it was really happening—her dream was really coming true, that he loved her as she loved him, passionately, without reservation, that he was making her wholly, completely his, and that his eyes, which she saw only fleetingly with each descent of her heaving bosom, which strained painfully against the tight stays of her bodice, were filled with desire for her—only

her, when suddenly they burst from their eyelets and zapped him
across the nose.   —*Barbara B. Shulman*
                                                    Palo Alto, Calif.

When Kimberly brushed out the auburn waves of her hair that
morning in a pool of Madrid sunshine, a few inconspicuous flakes
of confetti spilled to the bureau, causing her brain to be aswarm
with thoughts of last night's fiesta, especially irritation: who was
that dark, well-shouldered man who had sneered over her,
grasped *Zorba the Greek* protruding from her handbag, and
hurled—with the slight lisp of the true Spaniard—"I gather you
believe thith ith proper reading for a governeth"?
                                                    —*Mary Ann Singleton*
                                                    Soquel, Calif.

Groped thoroughly, Laurel Desmond cast her eyes over the
magnificent scenery of the historic Pacific Northwest and also
studied the tall, sandy-haired man with mocking eyes who'd ac-
costed her only after knocking her onto the imported Persian rug
in front of the hotel desk, then met her trembling lips with a ful-
filling kiss that demonstrated to her that the manners of a pushy
man varied inversely with his ability to divine her every secret
physical desire, nestled deeply within her heaving breast where
no other man had ever been able to probe. —*Patricia Lu Pillot*
                                                    Jersey Shore, Pa.

Her eyes were amazingly deep amber-like pools of falling starlight as he pulled her roughly to him while she struggled with all
her fragile might to disengage herself until his first kiss on her
alabaster throat had her hanging limp and faintish in his arms,
and his second kiss (a little farther down on the pulsating pulse of
her throat) had her emitting a series of noisome puppy-like

sounds, while his third kiss (still farther down) alerted her every sense, for she knew that—at any moment now—he could chance upon her falsies.
—*Pat Walker*
Garden Grove, Calif.

Under the cover of the night's merciless, icy downpour, Garth Tremaine moved stealthily yet gracefully toward the portico of the forbidding old mansion in which his beloved, the beautiful heiress Galatea D'Lanton, was purported to be held prisoner by her eccentric and alcoholic uncle, Jacob Slatter, cursing softly as yet another icy droplet found its way inside the collar of the opera cape he had flung hastily over his broad shoulders as he rushed to her rescue—quite forgetting, he realized ruefully, to notify the constable, or even to tell his mother not to expect him for dinner.
—*Linda C. Smurr*
Newton, Kans.

The sky pregnant with scudding mauve-tinted clouds did not distract Gwendillian, the dulcet-voiced wench from Boca Croza, who at this moment was crazed with scented passion, breasts heaving, eyes dilated, heart thudding, and lungs shouting, "Feona, you tart, you can't have Hubert!"
—*Dr. and Mrs. Morris Saperstein*
Highland, Calif.

The madwoman stood in the rear of the wedding, her fists clenching and unclenching in an extremity of grief, as the Lord Robert de Rocquefort, fourth earl of Camembert, stepped forward to the altar amidst the clamor of trumpets and the meeping of krummhorns to claim his soon-to-be bride, a lush and voluptuous bit of heaving-breasted cheesecake clad in billows of white "pearl de mer" satin, the brocading of which had claimed the sight of twelve village children, and the vision of which now broke the lowly madwoman's heart as she remembered how the Lord Rocquefort had first come upon her in the woods with his velvet britches down about his knees, and how she had dreamt of being the bride kneeling so happily beside him at the altar.

—*Jan Bender*
Los Angeles, Calif.

A gentle breeze ruffled the golden fingers of her hair, not unlike a tiny tadpole skipping through the strands, and the sun shone warm on her tan-filled face, yet still Amanda was troubled by a nagging suspicion that she could not clearly identify but could feel as palpably as she could feel her Piaget diamond-faced watch on her left wrist, a shapely wrist that sloped gently into a rounded forearm cloaked in—and then it came to her, and she finally knew that her feelings of discomfort had been caused by lingering doubt about the percentage of natural fiber in her favorite red sweater.

—*Chuck Bell*
Wichita, Kans.

Ignoring the slime as it dripped onto the gem-laden, barnacle-encrusted treasure chest they had chanced to discover, Jasmine wondered, as she secured the last of the twenty-four buttons on her satin bodice, if the daily splendors she sought in the hidden island caves, with her soul mate Raoul, were worth the bile-inducing nightly sacrifices she made in the century-old four-poster, with her poxied husband, Lord Rathbone . . .

—*Bitten Norman*
Baltimore, Md.

There was an ice blizzard on the morning of my arrival at Thererestone, an arrival long contemplated with a strange mix-

ture of wonder and trepidation, for legends and rumors about this great ancestral mansion had been woven into the warp and woof of my life since infancy; but now the crenelated ramparts gleamed and glistened like the palace of the Ice Queen herself, hung about with iridescent icicles encrusted with millions of flecks like gems in the diadem of the same frigid monarch, as trees and shrubs knelt in homage under tinkling shimmering coats of diamonds, touched by the lingering rays of the late-rising sun as by a magic wand, and the whole blinding symphony of chatoyant light captured my gaze as though I were witness to some celestial transfiguration and about to enter the portals of some enchanted kingdom—whereupon I alighted gracefully from the carriage onto a patch of black ice and fell ass over backward in the driveway, sustaining a compound fracture of the right tibia which was to keep me imprisoned in that dank moldy rathole of a house for the next eight months.   —*Carol A. Phillips*
Anchorage, Alaska

Flicking the ash of dying thoughts of Bernice off the tip of the cigar of his burning passion, he suspected that she (hopefully, of course, unintentionally, although he rather doubted it, preferring not to lie to himself, considering the duck) had spitefully tripped the fuse box of his heart one last (or perhaps, next to the last) time, plunging his light and happy heart into the inkiest blackest ebony of despair—could she have possibly, after all, ever loved him, wanted him, needed him, as desperately as he had imagined that he her—he, only a male governess, and she, a female Rochester, blind, disfigured, and married, but somehow, wildly attractive—he decided that she could.   —*Star Meyer*
Los Angeles, Calif.

"I despise you," Ravena said, her icy tone betrayed by her face contorted with conflicting hurt, rage, and adoration; then she flung herself helplessly against his lean but well-muscled body, not even noticing his curly chest hairs tickling her nose as her misery was sucked into an undertow by a rising tide of passion.
—*Mary Anne Linden*
Eugene, Oreg.

BILLY-BOB
GRINNED
IN PURE
DELIGHT

"A SPECTACULAR,
SPRAWLING NOVEL ABOUT A
FAMILY THAT DARED
TO PURSUE A VISION
—TO GET THEIR HANDS
ON EVERY SQUARE INCH OF
LAND IN THE TERRITORY."

Billy-Bob grinned in pure delight as he felt the "kerthump" of yet another Texas armadillo being flattened beneath the wheels of his green '63 Chevy pick-up truck with manual transmission and built-in fuzzy pink dice suspended from the rear-view mirror in which he could now see the flattened armadillo, stretched across the yellow dotted line bisecting the steaming asphalt, laughing in delight as Sheriff Kudzu's flaming pink Cadillac Seville's left front tire spun through armadillo guts, spewing an orangy-brown mess along the left putrid pink fender.

—*Debra M. Brewin-Wilson*
Edison, N.J.

The hungriest Caleb had ever been was the winter his pa swapped the shotgun for whiskey and the state closed off Highway 60 so they couldn't even pick up the occasional possum— sometimes still warm and steaming in the cold Georgia air—after the big trucks rumbled by.   —*David Willingham*
Georgetown, Tenn.

Remorselessly, Big Betty bellowed into the CB microphone, "EAT MY DUST, GOOD BUDDIES!" laughing derangedly as she peeled out of the chicken-shack truck stop, scowling ear to ear, popping gizzards into her fat face and leaving behind a trail of poultry carcasses (as gray foreboding clouds spewed frozen raindrops in her cautionless path, whetting her appetite for her favorite bedtime snack—pearl onions in clam sauce).

—*James Coffey*
St. Pete Beach, Fla.

With a bold, brazen swagger that belied the sheer idiocy of the act, Davin strode headlong into the hot wax chamber of Crazy Ollie's Economy Self-Serve Car 'n' Small Truck Wash, not un-

like a slaughterhouse swine charging snout-first into the unyielding path of one of those big metal things with handles—I forget what they call them—but it'd hurt like nobody's business to get slammed over the head with one, for the buff 'n' polishing of his foolish young life. —*Denny Guge*
Kearney, Nebr.

Seth "Big Horn" McCoy, the grizzled old mountain man who long ago single-handedly tamed this once wild wilderness, making it a safe and decent place to live, was overwhelmed with shame and rejection as he peered out his cabin window at the hundreds of settlers his brave and selfless pioneering labors had brought to this territory, and who now stood a quarter mile away, shouting their demand that he either take a bath or move to the other side of the mountain. —*Dennis McKiernan*
Louisville, Ky.

"I wouldn't be so paranoid if everybody wasn't persecuting me all the time," said Uncle Eugene to the other cotton pickers in the snowy white field, hitching up his bulging cotton sack, which trailed behind him like a giant white slug inching tremulously through the russet furrows. —*M. U. Griffin*
Huntsville, Ala.

Cindy Lou's decision to go on national TV when Mr. Charles Kuralt himself would be coming to broadcast the finals of the Upperchucky County Rutabaga Roundup she was queen of, and tell the whole world that Randy Joe, the son of that high-and-mighty Mr. Randolph Jukes III down at the Pinecrest Bank & Trust Co., was the father of the unborn secret she was harboring in her belly, took a load off her mind. —*Jack Tucker*
Berkeley, Calif.

Tentative spring dawn caressed the tips of Wheeler Crest with golden light as the newborn colt struggled to his hooves and surveyed the knee-high grass and fat cattle of Round Valley—cattle to be trucked to Los Angeles and then returned to Bishop as prime flank steaks for slow desiccation over smoldering mountain mahogany, making the best smoked jerky between the Continental and Great Western Divides; but this did not concern the colt as he took a first faltering step and toppled onto his fuzzy white-blazed nose.　　　　　　　　　　　　　　　*—Sandra L. Brock*
Squaw Valley, Idaho

Jock Berry chewed coal instead of breath mints, his pants were so tight they bounced radar, and his shoulders were like well-matched Buicks, but his weakness for Elvis and Ding-Dongs had kept him close to the family bait farm.　　　*—Patty Day Frasure*
Bakersfield, Calif.

The new day opened like a Walt Disney time-lapse film of a rose, revealing an endless field of cabbage, inhabited by one lonely farmer, clad in his underwear, crying, "The dawn has come, and with it, life!"　　　　　　　　　*—Jamie Brickhouse*
Beaumont, Tex.

I had left the barbecue quite hurriedly with sketchy directions to the ladies' room "out back," and now faced a black cow wearing one red earring, standing beneath an ill windmill, bladeless and bent from years of prevailing winds, and as she watched me with bovine detachment, my heels sank arch deep into the mire . . . I hate the country!　　　　　　　　　　*—Joan Gilliam*
Houston, Tex.

MORE
VILE
PUNS

"SWEPT BY PASSION,
BRUSHED BY DESIRE,
SHE WAS POLISHED OFF
BY LOVE."

To be fully appreciated, this story must be read in the nude—so, please, bare with me.
—*Michael McGarel*
Riverdale, Ill.

General Amaya, fifty-ish and porcine, had many stout followers.
—*Yvonne Foster*
Reston, Va.

"I suggest you stick to painting, Mr. Van Gogh—you sure don't have an ear for music."
—*Lee DiAngelo*
St. Petersburg, Fla.

It was her first job interview in years, and Dolores wept as she entered the headquarters of the Professional Mourners Association and read the large, tastefully lettered sign that said, "We Will Sell No Whine Before Its Time."
—*Larry D. Kohlhorst*
Sylvania, Ohio

Wally and Bea had some rather tiny problems to attend to, not the least of which was Minnie's school.
—*Lynne Marie Waldron*
San Jose, Calif.

"I've come to my wit's end," shouted the king as he carefully aimed his foot at the bent-over form of his court jester.
—*Helene Story*
Sacramento, Calif.

As he felt his final breath being crushed from him by the closing fronds of the genetically engineered giant Venus's fly-trap, its digestive enzymes now oozing down his arms and legs, Bif "Green Thumb" Radetsky, ace detective and part-time florist,

heard the evil botanist, Dr. I. M. A. Weed, laugh menacingly, "You see, Mr. Radetskey, Matilda's bite is worse than her bark!"
—*Clark Ochikubo*
Stanford, Calif.

After Marco Polo split the Mongol scene and went to Beverly Hills to open a new watering hole, unimaginatively called the Polo Lounge, Mrs. P. returned to Venice, took up with a scruffy little gondolier whom she affectionately dubbed "Pony," and enthusiastically began raising a large string of Polo Ponies.
—*Gary S. Dunbar*
Pacific Palisades, Calif.

How could this heel of a man gain such power in a tight-fitting company like Patterson's Podiatry Shoes when all he wore were wing tips and tennis sneakers? —*Sherry Licu*
Healdsburg, Calif.

"Peter the flasher wanted to retire, but then decided to stick it out for another year," he typed, but the keyboard mocked him cruelly so he said the hell with it and became a stockbroker.
—*Stephen Seitz*
Arlington, Va.

Phil and Rhonda Dendron thought that all of their troubles with their pet cobra "Furse" had been resolved by the famous snake veterinarian, Doctor Saltun Pepper, who assured them that "Furse" had been relieved of his desire to coil (not unlike the way cats and dogs become after having been deprived of their natural desires), but Paul was abruptly awakened by his wife that night when she screamed, "Furse is coiled again!!" —*Steve Jenne*
Springfield, Ill.

Hans Zumouth, the butcher of Düsseldorf, growing more and more desperate over the ever-dwindling supply of cheap meat in the peace-ravaged community, resorted to trapping birds for use as sausage-stuffing, then collapsed from the guilt of violating his sacred oath as a gastrophysicist, having taken a tern for the wurst.

—*John S. Flagg*
Lexington, Mass.

From the coffee-colored skies, rain dripped incessantly on the grounds of the deCroissant estate and on the upturned mugs of Link Sausage, private eye, and his girl friend Patti, who knew they had to split this case—deCroissant may have been totally flaky, but his French wife, Miette, had been the toast of three continents until someone (either deCroissant himself or possibly Miette's hard-boiled lover, Poche) had cracked under the pressure of shelling out for the lady's expensive tastes and had scrambled her brains sometime early on this tart spring morning, leaving Linck and Patti no choice but to grill both men before either had a chance to waffle his way out of the current jam.

—*Lynda Carraher*
Umatilla, Oreg.

Attorney Jack Grimm scrambled through his briefs, throwing them to the floor, until he found the gun tangled in his red bikinis.

—*Charlotte Townsend Springer*
Tallahassee, Fla.

Half-crazed by ravenous hunger and the primordial desire to survive, Rhett Butler seized the scrawny chicken leg, deaf to her entreaties to share the only food left in Atlanta, and snarled, "Frankly, Scarlett, I don't div a gam!"

—*Dennis J. Doolin*
Tokyo, Japan

It was the day that all drank their beer, stomped their stumpf-fiddles, and danced their polkas in celebration of the pork sausage that made the city famous, for it was Bratwurst Day, and all sizzled, including the "brats," in the early August heat—it was truly the best of days and the wurst of days.

—*Joel Valentincic*
Long Beach, Calif.

With her strength failing rapidly, the dying Augusta reached for her one night stand, her breast heaving coarsely, cancer having finally overtaken her, for the gilded framed memento of her dwarfish, undersized Norwegian explorer-lover, which slipped from her grasp and fell to the mosaic tile floor, shattering as she wheezed her last regret, "Alas, Leif was too short."

—*Stephanie Lashmet*
Scott Martin
Tom Sullivan
Newark, Del.

The picture was truly atrocious, a cacophony of color which grated painfully on the eyeballs, so no one was at all the least bit surprised when the museum director had it replaced on the moving van and shipped back to when it came, amid multitudinous cheers from the crowd . . . except for one man—when the local paper announced how happy everyone had been to see that van go, Vincent, carefully perusing it for the umpteenth time that day, mournfully shook his head and wondered if they would ever spell his name right.

—*Janet M. Kaul*
Redwood, Calif.

Fall had come to the city; the trees had turned to yellows and the winos had turned to reds.

—*James Ladwig*
Hoopa, Calif.

"He's lying," thought Inspector Brannigan, as the curator of ancient armor—quickly penetrating the disguises and fingering the two suspects in the lineup of international museum thieves—assured the burly officer, "The Austrian is behind the breastplate, and the Czech is in the mail."
—*Jack Tucker*
Berkeley, Calif.

It was tragic carnage requiring an autopsy and the coroner's report revealed that "two huge bears, a female and a male, had devoured the fishermen, a Russian and a Czechoslovakian, and it was determined that the Russian was eaten by the female while the Czech was in the male."
—*Dave Kessler*
New Paris, Ohio

"Gee, darling, is that Darjeeling?" infused Earl Grey, teasingly.
—*Robert Michael Jackson*
Sacramento, Calif.

A CLEAR-CUT CASE OF HOMICIDE

"A CONSOLE OF
CONTEMPORARY NIGHTMARES
AT WHICH THE AUTHOR
FINGERS EVERY
SINISTER KEY,
AND WORKS THE
PEDALS LIKE CRAZY."

"A clear-cut case of homicide," muttered Police Detective Ace Wiley, teeth clenched on the ever-present unlit cigar, as he viewed the twenty-four bodies neatly stacked like cordwood in the narthex of the Faith Baptist Church, each with a small black hole in the right temple.   —*Al Schmiess*
Jamestown, N.D.

Ignoring his palpitating prostate, Chief Inspector Merde Alors crawled through the slimy sewers of Paris in search of clues to the mysterious disappearance of Sir Cedric Fey, head of the British Secret Service, who was last seen attempting to drink absinthe through his nose at the Moulin Rouge.   —*Bill Sweeney*
Santa Rosa, Calif.

"This is a bust!" she yelled, as she ripped open her coat, boldly displaying her ample authority.   —*R. J. Wilcsek*
San Diego, Calif.

It was quite simple, Dr. Blackthorn mused, "The green jelly bean had obviously been bitten in half during the violent struggle for the petard, and the strand of flax found under the victim's left armpit could only have come from the spinning of that ancient and quite mad old crone (who, incidentally, is Marguerite's grandmother, a Mrs. Helmsly, who resides in Twilight Manor, a nursing home in a small, picturesque mining town, Pontrillyln-bragnathy, in Wales—the very same village the victim had been posted to during the Great War, having cruelly left a certain young, and rather plain, Miss Danbury, enceinte and bereft, whom we know later plunged into the darkly swirling waters of Dunwich Loch on that fateful day).   —*Ann Berger*
Tustin, Calif.

The suicidal killer crept around the corner with his double-edged sword ready to swing at the first attractive floral print sundress.

—*David L. Baker*
Georgetown, Ky.

As the police chief led me into the kitchen, I could see that her face was pitched forward into a boiled pot of homemade chicken soup—stewing in her own juices, as it were.

—*Martha Simpson*
Glastonbury, Conn.

The lovable but red-eyed pooch ceased foaming at the mouth, the parrot poked an oddly shaped object back under the birdseed, and the recently widowed Mr. Carbolic abruptly shooed the children upstairs, but their reaction to her surprise arrival with a gift of steaming casserole did not arouse suspicion in Miss Styles.

—*Patty Day Frasure*
Bakersfield, Calif.

"You'll think me a potty old lady, I know," Miss Mumble burbled as she cut another slice of bread, slathered it with good Devon butter, and took a thoughtful bite, "but I'm not the least surprised that eleven people have died oddly at Wistwander Ponders, since murder is so simple that one has only to . . ." but then she toppled gently off the chintz chair, since the vicar had put cadmium in the bread, the butter, her shawl, her shoes, the tea, her fluffy white wig, her woolens, and the chintz chair.

—*Gretchen S. Ellis*
Houston, Tex.

'Twas in the middle of the morning that Eulalie, awakened by the mournful dirge of her dear lately departed husband's pet cats

and mules (who would not leave his body unattended, even though there was hardly room for them all on the front porch, where the coffin conveniently awaited pickup from the Cloudtop Memorial Park), looked up and saw her husband's favorite gold-plated golf putter—the missing murder weapon, as it turned out—slowly circling above her, attached to the bedroom ceiling fan.
—*Mary Wilkes Towner*
Urbana, Ill.

After a courting couple strolling across Hamlet-upon-Rye's town common had stumbled onto the first corpse, pierced through the heart with the stake from the "Please Curb Your Dog" notice, the Chief Constable, Col. Sir Duncan Wright-Ffoule, was confident his local men could discover the perpetrator; but when the first corpse was soon followed by a second, spun-dry in the launderette on Market Street, Sir Duncan reflected that perhaps it was time Scotland Yard should be called in.
—*Lucy Shores*
Hartford, Conn.

Had I but known then what lay before me—my discovery of Aunty Tibby's terrible secret and of the headless ten-year-old corpse so cleverly concealed behind the set of Richard Harding Davis in the library, the gruesome crossbow suicide of one of my dearest childhood friends, and my own close brush with death on that rainswept nightmarish night, which left me a nerve-shattered cripple with therapy bills not covered by my medical insurance— I might not have gone to spend Christmas with the Whitleys.
—*L. H. Sintetos*
Santa Cruz, Calif.

LYTTONY IV

"FROM BANANA DAIQUIRIS TO BONZO THE CHIMP AND FROM SIDNEY LONGSTREET TO THE FIRST ALL-FEMALE LAND SURVEY."

"I'd rather have a frontal lobotomy than a bottle in front of me," snarled Tee-total Tex, twisting his moustache into a caricature of the man that the world would one day recognize as John Wayne, at which point Crazy Horse withdrew the bottle of vintage Beaujolais for the last time, surveyed the sea of cavalry dead, and called for his favorite tomahawk (the one with the Velcro-covered handle).
—*Steve Havens*
Chicago, Ill.

Trail boss was not a job to be taken lightly, Logan knew, as it meant rising long before dawn, with the frost still on the prairie and the corn flowers, then setting the wagoners to rights, the coffee brewing, the women and children stirring, the oxen feeding, and finally hitching up and rolling the Conestogas, but, ah, the sheep!
—*Terrence Carroll*
San Jose, Calif.

The whirling blades of a dust-encrusted fan whispered their airy hum over the occasional low muttering that could be heard from one of the barflies sprawled on the high, heavily duct-taped, vinyl-covered, padded stools at the far end of the polished bar, lazily stirring the smoky haze that hung, wraith-like, over their glistening pates and sweaty, stained, undershirt-clad torsos enveloped in the sweltering Carolina heat, so humid tonight that its very heaviness belied the barely concealed electric tension of the scene, as Trevor, bone-weary from the seemingly endless miles of pine-fringed blacktop he had traversed that day, his pack slung loosely from his narrow shoulders, stumbled haltingly across the sagging floor toward the dumpy barmaid staring disconsolately into the warm beer at her elbow in a half-drained glass smudged by the cerise lipstick she had slashed across her coarse face, poked aside the soppy wet bar rag, carefully eased himself onto an empty bar stool, and gasped in a hoarse but obviously refined English accent, "Sidney Longstreet is dead!"

—*Rod Briggs*
Seal Beach, Calif.

On a gray and rainy day, during "that Texan's" administration, a Noble Experiment in public land management brought two blushing, virginal, recent graduates of an Eastern liberal arts college to the wilds of western Oregon, one carrying a surveyor's theodolite, the other on the end of a measuring chain, an ax in one hand frantically hacking at the great mass of rhododendron and maple, entwined with poison ivy which blocked their goal of reaching the summit of the highest mountain range in the West, completing the first all-female survey in United States history.

—*John Gumert*
Santa Fe, N.M.

The road carried the morning stage from Jasper toward Bad Fork like the hand of a long, dusty god with cactus and tumbleweed whiskers flowing under a huge blue-eye-sky that held a twinkling pupil-sun blazing at its center like a spark thrown from a coach wheel spun against granite not unlike the hard face of the driver who lashed his whip at the six-horse team, screaming, "I'll burn the rims off the wheels and come in rollin' on spokes."

—*John Balkwill*
Hampton, Va.

When the massive steel doors crashed open, revealing Widget, the midget, ex–chicken hawk, pimp of Locust Street, previous Mini-Lightweight Champion of the World mud-wrestler, sometime dope dealer, occasional bouncer of teen night clubs, onetime square dance caller at homes for unwed mothers, Chinese

food connoisseur, filthy book critic, diamond-level Amway businessman, and an all around nice guy—naked—even he knew this was totally out of character.
—*Donna Hurth*
San Jose, Calif.

"Manganese!!" Old Dutch screamed, dropping his pickax and spooking his faithful ass, Isabel, who stumbled and fell a mile and a half, four-legged freestyle, to the bottom of Hell's Jagged Canyon, landing with a faint, plaintive whinny and a horrifying "plop" that echoed halfway to Nevada as Old Dutch watched in stunned amazement, pausing to wonder if a fresh vein of ore was worth the life of the only woman he ever loved.
—*E. Von Pond*
Stratford, Conn.

"The train passed by here," said the Indian scout, a tall, well-muscled Sioux with a weathered, dark red face, hawk-like eyes, and a history of gastronomic troubles, who paused to further study the ground at his feet (ground which would someday be part of the state of North Dakota), "and it traveled recently, for I can still see its tracks."
—*Michael McGarel*
Riverdale, Ill.

A saddle-weary Cactus Sam smashed the glass down on the bar of the Two-Gun Saloon and said, with barely controlled fury, "This Banana Daiquiri is not sweet enough!"
—*Richard C. Johnson*
Honolulu, Hawaii

The cowboys were hot and tired from the long drive, the past two weeks having been the hardest men had ever known, but

tomorrow looked to be better—tomorrow they would try it with
horses.   —*Amy M. Yamakawa*
Honolulu, Hawaii

"This land has been ours," sternly intoned the Indian Chief-
tain Sneaks-Around-Quietly-in-the-Dark, "since the world was
created and the Great Spirit sold it to us for eleven kilograms of
sulphur dyes; and you palefaces have signed a treaty stating that
it is ours as long as the grass grows atop the buffaloes, as the
beans fly south for the winter, as the fish chant maledictions at
the unfeeling sky, as the mangy horses chew the fat with the
sluggish squirrels and the mechanical albatross of the night, as
the iridescent wombats catch cold from the undercooked pasta
served them by the Great Spirit, aye, as long as the world as we
know it continues to exist!—so by what legal right do you try to
take it from us?   —*Bard Bloom*
Cambridge, Mass.

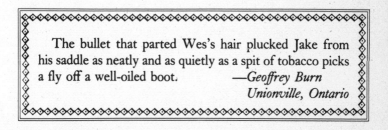

The bullet that parted Wes's hair plucked Jake from
his saddle as neatly and as quietly as a spit of tobacco picks
a fly off a well-oiled boot.   —*Geoffrey Burn*
Unionville, Ontario

Finally, and at long last, it was the moment that every man,
woman, and child on the planet earth had been waiting for (well,
everyone but Marvin Finstermyer, who had been oblivious to the
world in general for the last twenty-two years, ever since he had
been accidentally lobotomized when he got his head stuck in the

bars of his crib and his brother Harold had tried to extricate him with an attempt to narrow his skull, in order to pull him loose, by using his father's vise-grip pliers—the ones that sometimes refused to release whatever they were holding), the moment when they would learn what really happened to Bonzo the Chimp.

—*Teresa Boxleitner*
Moscow, Idaho

MUFFY
AND THE
KGB

"A SHOCKING WEB OF HATRED,
GREED, TYRANNY, INJUSTICE,
WAR, THEFT, MURDER, LYING,
TREACHERY, TORTURE,
HUNGER, SUFFERING, AND
INCREDIBLE RUDENESS."

Escaping from KGB headquarters was the easy part, but Muffy knew that more than stealth would be needed to get her past the border guards back to West Berlin in a madras blouse, a tan skirt, and Gucci loafers, so she employed guile and daring, breezily striding up to the surprised sentries and pleasantly inquiring with a sunny smile, "Anybody want to buy a copy of *Mohammed Speaks?* A Ronco Vegamatic? Greatest Hits of Wayne Newton? White Cloverine Brand Salve? No? What about those imperialist lackeys across the bridge? Yes? Great! Be back in a minute; don't bother to lower the barrier, only be a sec—no big deal, thanks guys, really." —*Robert D. Norris, Jr.*
Tulsa, Okla.

Grabbing the vice consul's teenage daughter in the green shantung skirt from behind as she stepped out of the Otis automatic elevator, the swarthy, husky kidnapper clapped a chloroform-soaked linen pocket-handkerchief over her mouth and nose, preventing her from screaming, and thwarting her writhing, contorted struggle for air and freedom or from merely attracting notice from anyone in the periphery of the hotel lobby, filled with a number of persons from all walks of life and of diverse ages, who could have been her potential rescuers, and had the kidnap not been obscured behind two fake-but-realistic sego palms used for hotel lobby decor, and had the assault not been perpetrated so swiftly and forcefully by this assailant-for-hire, who was known in the slang of the underworld as a "muff-man"!

—*Ralph S. Marks*
Houston, Tex.

The sudden shock of capture by the KGB of Britain's top MI-5 agent within the still darkened hangar shook Toddy McDonald since the aircraft's instruments had confirmed he covertly com-

mandeered a state-of-the-art Backfire Bomber undetected from East Germany to Belgium; but it now became humiliatingly clear to him that the cockpit he so stealthily crawled into was nothing more than a mere flight simulator. —*Frank R. Adams III*
Pensacola, Fla.

As the singer, a tone-deaf Bulgarian with a voice like flat Guinness, poured his song into the ears of the vile patrons of der Kister, Hamburg's filthiest, smokiest, and most outrageous low-life bar, Hunter—sensing that his man was suddenly close—slid his hand slowly and unobtrusively into his jacket, wrapping his fingers deftly around the butt and through the trigger guard of his 9mm automatic—as he had done so many times before—and shot himself rather nastily in the left thigh.

—*Geoffrey Burn*
Unionville, Ontario

Wexel Goughball was a dedicated, Class A agent for the Company, which meant he could wire a Rhode Island Red for sound and plastique; maim a guy at 30 feet with six-inch raw macaroni and a spitball; manufacture a passport from recycled W-2 forms; qualify in 36 different weapons, including putty knife, lethal swizzlestick, and the Joker from a deck of cards; and, in fact, had decapitated a bad guy with a standard-size business card lifted from a false East German nuclear physicist in the lobby of the UN Building. —*William D. Cox*
San Francisco, Calif.

They came at him from both sides at once, the Greek with a sapper, the Turk with his nasty curved blade, and it crossed his mind that nothing had gone right that morning—the milk on his cereal was blinky, his newspaper was torn from the way the boy

hurled it, one of his laces broke, and he was wearing one black and one brown shoe, strictly against the department's neatness policy—and now this.
—*Charlotte Mortimer*
Ramona, Calif.

He had traveled the continent, leaving the corpse of a narcoleptic Croatian nationalist in a Hefty Steel Sack on the streets of Karachi, not to mention that Macedonian diamond smuggler entombed in a massive wedge of feta on a tanker bound for Brooklyn, he reflected as he took another suck at his last Vicegrip 100.
—*Daniel Rich*
Fort Lee, N.J.

Moscow can be a pretty cold kind of place, especially in winter, that's why I was glad I'd struck up a conversation with Gennady when he playfully flicked a graying and painfully worn bath towel at me in the men's changing room at the Moskva River Polar Bears Swimming Club.
—*Matthew Cope*
Outremont, Quebec

"Gentlemen," the admiral addressed his Pentagon colleagues, "we face a grave danger—I have just learned that the enemy possesses a new Brastron Bomb atomic warhead which, when detonated, destroys all brass, leaving more valuable human resources untouched . . . just kidding!"
—*Mary T. Neal*
Toronto, Ontario

BUSBY
BRAITHWAITE
DOES
ALPHA
CENTAURI

"A BREATHLESS STORY
THAT ZIPS ALONG
AT WARP SPEED . . .
BECAUSE THE
CHARACTERS ARE
UNDEVELOPED AND THE
AUTHOR HAS NOT
THE LEAST SENSE
OF NARRATIVE PACE."

Busby Braithwaite stepped out of his single-seater spacecraft on the sixth planet of Alpha Centauri and looked up at the hideous creature flapping around above his head, craning its long neck to get a better look at him and then going into paroxysms of uncontrollable laughter, making Busby wonder whether he too should laugh or cry at this first form of disconcertingly intelligent life encountered on the new planet.   —*Alec Kitroeff*
Psychico, Greece

Malibu, leader of the peasant rebellion on Beachwear IV, stood on the lip of the hill and watched the laser cannon's flaming tongue lick a black line of decay across the jagged teeth of the castle towers and urged his ocean of followers to the assault ladders with the cry, "Serfs UP!"   —*Michael Miller*
Fresno, Calif.

Billions of light years away there exists a small, insignificant planet, insignificant because this story takes place in South Jersey during the Great Depression.   —*Thomas Corrigan*
Seymour, Conn.

"Chortle, chortle!" lisped Drek Zorchkov, arch-villain of a thousand galaxies, as he began to spray the lovely legs of Cynthia Come Nicely with Xttilian hair remover, "nobody can shave you now!"   —*Robin Wood*
Pinole, Calif.

Suddenly the truth hit me: this wasn't the earth—but worse, the woman I had taken all these years to be my mother was not my mother at all; she was Gogi Grant, possibly the hottest singing star of the '50s, and, furthermore, the uniformed man ticketing my car was also clearly not who he pretended to be—just what kind of a sap was I being taken for?

—*Dennis Kaplan*
San Francisco, Calif.

With rising lust, Zabor Son of Hathora, Prince of the Magador, Lord Protector of Midax, and Shaman of the Incunabula, eagerly followed the nubile maiden as she stepped onto the deserted platform, hardly aware of the sagging brown socks beneath the grimy trench coat.

—*Charles Goldberg*
Titusville, N.J.

He had been crawling through the burned-out waste for a bleak eternity of neverdays, or it may only have been an hour, when a sound of machinery that could never exist again in the ruins of what was once a bustling farm lot buzzed in his ears, or did it? and he realized it was the humming alarm on his digital watch calling him to a lunch date he was going to miss for the rest of his life, which meant until about two o'clock if his estimates of his radiation dosage were correct.

—*Jaye Moretz*
Pleasant Hill, Calif.

Dr. Glenda Holcombe, interplanetary sex therapist, blew a strand of her immaculately coiffed platinum blond hair with a quick breath from her eyes, and addressed Dr. Ferguson: "This is going to be an interesting planet, Fergie; I thought this was a rubber glove, and now you tell me that it's a Blodkinoid condom!"

—*Richard Clopton*
Alameda, Calif.

"The worst thing about preparing gleedon eggs," Cadet Spencer mused, "was getting all the hnork spit off," while in the other compartment, gentle Esther Threadwicke put the silver polish back and beamed warmly at the fresh, clean tray of cat-neutering tools.
—*John Thompson*
Cully Abrell
Peck, Kans.

"Damn the Saurian brandy! Warp speed astern!" yelled the chief engineer, the flip of his kilt answering an age-old question as he leapt over the body of his fallen captain.
—*Pauline M. Johnson*
Los Altos, Calif.

We'd made it through yet another nuclear winter and the lawn had just trapped and eaten its first robin.
—*Kyle J. Spiller*
Garden Grove, Calif.

Mylar feared the dark, slobbering minions of the ophite master, the Serpent Lord Sessala, who breathed the terror of solitudes and inspired the Goblin Fires to walk the night belching naphtha flames against the mile-high cardboard walls of Baras-lugg, the fortress city of the Geeks.
—*Daniel Rich*
Fort Lee, N.J.

As she artfully adjusted the lamé breast cups and golden gauze which comprised her luncheon outfit, Fourseas Breck felt certain that if that oily, self-proclaimed vegetarian Xaar Glenn Blen, ruler of the Nth world, served her another of those thick, gamey steaks cloned from his inner thigh, she would blow her lunch, if not her cover.

—Constance Clark Reese
San Francisco, Calif.

The tiny spaceship sputtered into view over the blue-pink horizon of Disney World (which was of course founded a millennium ago by refugees of Epcot Center) and after a momentary lurch and thud landed on the greenish-blue springy turf, but unfortunately this immediately killed all the natives of the planet, who looked exactly like garden variety earth grass.

—Mandy Slater
Kanata, Ontario

The slime-green appendage suckingly worked its way under the satin blanket and rippled along the sheets, staining them with a putrid ooze, streaked by the cancerous scabby warts that pimpled its surface, until it reached the unblemished ivory-like naked body of Candice, where it hesitated, gathering itself for the final scum-smearing surge toward her innocence, when she rolled away from it suddenly, muttering, "I told you I had a headache!"

—Michael A. O'Neill
Rohnert Park, Calif.

As she walked along in her innocent but sexy fashion, each of her firm young breasts bouncing in its own well-separated trajectory, the concealed alien leaped out in ambush, entwining slimy wet tentacles about her nubile limbs and dragging her backward into the darkness of the mud-pits of lost Atlantis while her fading scream terminated in a sharp gurgle.

—Bryan Gregory Stephenson
Seattle, Wash.

Sixteen-year-old Tracy Pechuco shook her head wildy in disbelief as she began the recount: "I know I didn't have six toes on my feet this morning!" she screamed, her voice trembling with terror as her brother Phil sat quietly grinning in the closet watching her tail begin to appear at the bottom of her dress.

—*Larry Sherman*
Hayward, Calif.

Malaena saw it at once ... pulsating, purulent in its liquid shape, filling her with an icy revulsion, yet she knew in her heart that, by the rising of the sun, her bronzed, glistening shape would be writhing in torment for the want of it, for Thojhma the Sheep God had inhaled the wafting incense, and nodded approvingly as the sacrificial altar gleamed redly in the flickering dawnlight, for even as she struggled, her body—throbbing with the need for mind bond—allowed her tingling tongue to call its name— "Ralph!!! Ralph!!!"

—*Angela Haw*
Olympia, Wash.

"I think nuns are good, too," Vigore agreed with his greenish tablemate, wiping a track of grease from the edge of his maw with the back of a seven-fingered hand, "they don't get stuck in me teeth like fishermans do."

—*J. Carlisle*
New York, N.Y.

"Oh, God, no, not again!" Jessica cried as for the fourth time that week, agonizing spasms wracked her body, inexorably turning her into a giant slug that would ravenously and mercilessly prey upon the halt, the weak, and the helpless until her shameful madness had passed—a madness that forced her, upon her re-

transformations, to retrace her steps, armed with J-Cloths, furtively erasing the telltale slime trail that could lead Detective Hugo to her door.   *—Libby Setkowicz*
Westmount, Quebec

Nydia found one of the drawbacks of being a werewolf was coming into heat during a full moon and later giving birth to decituplets.   *—R. W. O'Bryan*
Perrysburg, Ohio

SUDDEN TURNS

"HIS SAVAGE KISS
AROUSED HER SPIRIT,
HIS BOLD TOUCH
AWAKENED HER FLESH,
HIS STEAMY EMBRACE
ENFLAMED HER RASH."

Inga's breath came in ragged gasps as Virgil deftly manipulated her roseate flesh—each touch of his huge but knowing fingers sending delicious quiverings through her highly sensitized nerve endings, and she bit her knuckle, fearful that at any moment she might give way to sobs of raw animal pleasure; this, then, was love, she realized, as Virgil rubbed cool white gobs of Noxema onto her sunburned back.   *—Lynne Marie Waldron*
San Jose, Calif.

Sleeping, David thought, she was a sight to behold (and indeed she was!) and held his longing gaze upon her body, tracing every rise of the mounds of her supple flesh under the steamy bedsheets until slowly, slowly, slowly, very slowly, she languidly opened her gray-green eyes because they were, after all, stuck together from the gunk of her eye infection.   *—Elena Cáceres*
Stockton, Calif.

Ghost of the tule marches, wraiths of fog slithered over canal banks and seethed from dank sloughs' still cattails, slowly rising like steam from the extinct grizzlies' backs, like softly snorted breath of vanished tule elk, like smoke from extinguished but normally slow-burning Yokuts' fires, misty miasma inexorably writhed across the San Joaquin, reclaiming the man-altered valley for an evening, returning it to the spirits of its long dispossessed owners, and really fouling up traffic in Fresno.

—Sandra Brock
Squaw Valley, Calif.

A conscience is a loathsome thing, God wot, so it wasn't more than an hour later that I was wishing I hadn't slit Martin's throat.
—Marjorie Murch Stanley
Youngstown, Ohio

"The simple things in life are oft the most enriching," mused Lady Ashton as she nailed the squealing piglet to her Chesterfield.
                                                                                    —*Scott Davis Jones*
                                                                                    Sausalito, Calif.

As the hurricane-force storm moved rapidly toward shore, with its black clouds boiling like so much acrid smoke belching from a rendering plant smokestack and its winds causing the waves to claw at the breakwater like the nails of a child after a patch of poison ivy-infected skin, Chelsea dashed across the beach toward the only shelter she could find, a crab-infested niche in the rocks, thinking to herself, "Crap, there goes my thirty-dollar hairdo!"
                                                                                    —*Wanda Nevans*
                                                                                    Iola, Kans.

A small whimper of pleasure escaped unbidden from her provocative, bee-stung lips as his gleaming, sinewy body pressed ever closer, his hand snaking sensuously under the voluminous folds of her diaphanous mantilla and his face contorting venomously as it had done so many times before when he had fondled the split ends of her ragged mohawk.   —*Ann Ragland Bowns*
                                                                                    Carmichael, Calif.

The rushing cool breeze in hair and the sudden relief from all her worries and problems gave her the same glorious feeling of freedom she felt at sixteen when riding in Nick's convertible on the way to Sandy Hook State Park on a summer afternoon with the picnic basket and her new swimsuit bought just that morning at Selzer's department store, save the distinct difference of the rocky ground now rising rapidly to meet her, only because the drive to the beach lasted considerably longer than her jump from the canyon rim.
                                                                                    —*Will Conway*
                                                                                    Dover, N.H.

Sylvia's skin was exquisite, soft and pearly; Leonard loved the way it looked tacked on his wall.

—*Cynthia Conyers*
Aguanga, Calif.

"There's more than one way to skin a cat," Lydia thought, as she nailed the little paws to the dissection board.

—*Richard Deming*
Ventura, Calif.

A DARK AND STORMY NIGHT

AND NOW A WORD FROM OUR SPONSOR:

"IT WAS A DARK AND STORMY NIGHT; THE RAIN FELL IN TORRENTS—EXCEPT AT OCCASIONAL INTERVALS, WHEN IT WAS CHECKED BY A VIOLENT GUST OF WIND WHICH SWEPT UP THE STREETS (FOR IT IS IN LONDON THAT OUR SCENE LIES), RATTLING ALONG THE HOUSETOPS AND FIERCELY AGITATING THE SCANTY FLAME OF THE LAMPS THAT STRUGGLED AGAINST THE DARKNESS."

—Opening sentence of *Paul Clifford* (1830)

It was a dark and stormy night, and rolling clouds raced across a lowering firmament, frenzied by a screaming wind that clawed the rain from their tortured, turgid bowels and sent it lashing to the sodden, sullen earth that quivered below.

(from *The Last Days of Pomposity*)   *—M. S. Maire*
Cohasset, Mass.

It was a dark and stormy night, scary, even scarier when the lights went out 'til someone found some candles and our faithful butler, Bulwer, lit one.   *—Vern Orr*
San Pablo, Calif.

It was a dark and stormy night and the rain eventually turned into a steady drizzle not unlike the spray that comes from those flat, green garden hoses that have thousands of tiny holes on one side, except that it appeared to come from the sky rather than the ground.   *—Dennis McKiernan*
Louisville, Ky.

As pledges went, he was a stark and dormy knight: sullen house reps bombarded him continually with the virtues of their respective fraternities, integral occasions thus excepting, when he was cast upon by turgid preppies who crept about the hallways (for it is in Princeton that our scene lies), chatting to each other, while lettermen fiercely agitated the scanty frames of struggling cheerleaders, hoping to light their internal lamps and snuggle against their pom-poms.   *—Marc Schwarz*
San Mateo, Calif.

It was about 11 P.M., Central Standard Time (our story taking place within the boundaries of that particular time zone) and due to a cold front off the Rockies meeting up with a warm front off the Great Lakes there was heavy precipitation in the form of rain, winds gusting up to forty miles per hour, and generally low visibility, or in other words, it was a dark and stormy night.

—*Moses Montgomery*
Winnipeg, Manitoba

It was a dark and stormy night when Officer Blaney was summoned to the scene of a four-car accordion-type collision on the Toluca Lake off-ramp of the Hollywood Freeway which was culminated by a Ford pickup with the red, white, and blue mud flaps rear-ending the gray Pontiac Phoenix which had crinkled the left rear fender of the red Mercedes that had crashed into the yellow Honda Civic with the "If you can read this, thank a teacher" bumper sticker, but it was later in court, with the revelation that Lance Carrington, the driver of the Mercedes, had just flunked his senior English exam, that the possibility of "assault with a deadly weapon" became a possibility.   —*Eleanor Lyang*
San Jose, Calif.

It was a park, and Normy Wright felt he belonged there among the snow-tipped tulips, hanging down their heads, calm; duly noting the woolly caterpillars, resembling the pileous growth above his upper lip, except that it lacked all those tiny, pink feet.   —*Peggy Ryan*
Jacksonville, N.C.

The sunset plunged over the austere dormitories of the St. Edwards Boys School and slithered over the school's Scottish golf course; it was a stark and dormy night.   —*Robin Wood*
Pinole, Calif.

It was a stark and dormy night, just nine months since the twenty-four-hour power outage at Atascadero State University; now the sky was filled with stout-billed pinkish birds, ominously circling the university medical center with pink and blue swaddling bundles carefully cuddled, in the usual manner, beneath their mighty beaks.
—*S. Robert Tunick*
Los Angeles, Calif.

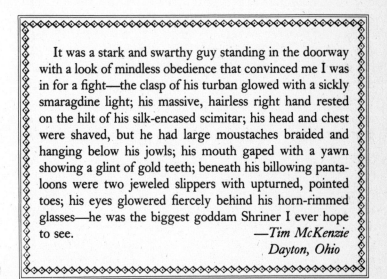

It was a stark and swarthy guy standing in the doorway with a look of mindless obedience that convinced me I was in for a fight—the clasp of his turban glowed with a sickly smaragdine light; his massive, hairless right hand rested on the hilt of his silk-encased scimitar; his head and chest were shaved, but he had large moustaches braided and hanging below his jowls; his mouth gaped with a yawn showing a glint of gold teeth; beneath his billowing pantaloons were two jeweled slippers with upturned, pointed toes; his eyes glowered fiercely behind his horn-rimmed glasses—he was the biggest goddam Shriner I ever hope to see.
—*Tim McKenzie*
Dayton, Ohio

®

Grand Prize from Apple Computer, Inc.
Macintosh™ 512K and MacWrite™ word processing software

ENTER THE BULWER-LYTTON
FICTION CONTEST

The Bulwer-Lytton Fiction Contest is an annual event that asks entrants to compose the worst possible opening sentence to a novel. Anyone anywhere may enter. The rules are simple:

1) Sentences may be of any length and entrants may submit more than one, but all entries must be original and previously unpublished.
2) Entries will be judged by categories, from "general" to detective, western, science fiction, romance, and so on. There will be overall winners as well as category winners.
3) Entries should be submitted on index cards, the sentence on one side and the entrant's name, address, and phone number on the other.
4) The deadline is April 15 (chosen because Americans associate it with another painful submission).

Send your entries to: Bulwer-Lytton Fiction Contest
Department of English
San Jose State University
San Jose, CA 95192-0090